INFORMATION TECHNOLOGY

RESEARCH,

INNOVATION,

and

E-Government

Committee on Computing and Communications Research to
Enable Better Use of Information Technology in Government

Computer Science and Telecommunications Board

Division on Engineering and Physical Sciences

National Research Council

NATIONAL ACADEMY PRESS
Washington, D.C.

NATIONAL ACADEMY PRESS   2101 Constitution Avenue, N.W. Washington DC 20418

NOTICE: The project that is the subject of this report was approved by the Governing Board of the National Research Council, whose members are drawn from the councils of the National Academy of Sciences, the National Academy of Engineering, and the Institute of Medicine. The members of the committee responsible for the report were chosen for their special competences and with regard for appropriate balance.

Support for this project was provided by the National Science Foundation under Grant No. EIA-9809120 and by the National Aeronautics and Space Administration. Any opinions, findings, conclusions, or recommendations expressed in this publication are those of the authors and do not necessarily reflect the views of the sponsors.

Cover: Photo courtesy of the U.S. Department of Agriculture Photo Library.

International Standard Book Number 0-309-08401-6

Library of Congress Control Number: 2002105188

Additional copies of this report are available from:

National Academy Press
2101 Constitution Ave., N.W.
Box 285
Washington, DC 20418
800-624-6242
202-334-3313 (in the Washington metropolitan area)
http://www.nap.edu

THE NATIONAL ACADEMIES

National Academy of Sciences
National Academy of Engineering
Institute of Medicine
National Research Council

The **National Academy of Sciences** is a private, nonprofit, self-perpetuating society of distinguished scholars engaged in scientific and engineering research, dedicated to the furtherance of science and technology and to their use for the general welfare. Upon the authority of the charter granted to it by the Congress in 1863, the Academy has a mandate that requires it to advise the federal government on scientific and technical matters. Dr. Bruce M. Alberts is president of the National Academy of Sciences.

The **National Academy of Engineering** was established in 1964, under the charter of the National Academy of Sciences, as a parallel organization of outstanding engineers. It is autonomous in its administration and in the selection of its members, sharing with the National Academy of Sciences the responsibility for advising the federal government. The National Academy of Engineering also sponsors engineering programs aimed at meeting national needs, encourages education and research, and recognizes the superior achievements of engineers. Dr. Wm. A. Wulf is president of the National Academy of Engineering.

The **Institute of Medicine** was established in 1970 by the National Academy of Sciences to secure the services of eminent members of appropriate professions in the examination of policy matters pertaining to the health of the public. The Institute acts under the responsibility given to the National Academy of Sciences by its congressional charter to be an adviser to the federal government and, upon its own initiative, to identify issues of medical care, research, and education. Dr. Kenneth I. Shine is president of the Institute of Medicine.

The **National Research Council** was organized by the National Academy of Sciences in 1916 to associate the broad community of science and technology with the Academy's purposes of furthering knowledge and advising the federal government. Functioning in accordance with general policies determined by the Academy, the Council has become the principal operating agency of both the National Academy of Sciences and the National Academy of Engineering in providing services to the government, the public, and the scientific and engineering communities. The Council is administered jointly by both Academies and the Institute of Medicine. Dr. Bruce M. Alberts and Dr. Wm. A. Wulf are chairman and vice chairman, respectively, of the National Research Council.

Preface

The emergence of the Internet and other electronic-commerce technologies has fundamentally altered the environment in which government delivers services to citizens, businesses, and other government entities. New expectations—that government will match the private sector in offering direct, rapid, round-the-clock access to information and services—are cultivating the growth of "e-government": the application of information technology (IT) and associated changes in agency practices to develop more responsive, efficient, and accountable government operations while fostering a more informed and engaged citizenry.

The role of government with respect to IT research, development, and use has also been shifting. The private sector has eclipsed government leadership in many areas of IT adoption and use, even as government continues in its critical role as the principal agent for long-term IT basic research and innovation. Much like their counterparts in the private sector, many in government are actively experimenting with exploiting the new technologies to improve operations and the delivery of services. A wide range of ideas is emerging from these experiments, contributing to technology development, the improvement of business practices, a more streamlined government, and a more sophisticated public. Following September 11, 2001, a new mission, homeland defense, is placing new demands on IT capabilities and is heightening interest in such related areas as critical infrastructure protection.

As part of its Digital Government research program, the National Science Foundation (NSF) requested that the Computer Science and Telecommunications Board (CSTB) undertake a study of how IT research could contribute more effectively to the activities and operations of government. CSTB established the Committee on Computing and Communications Research to Enable Better Use of Information Technology in Government to explore promising research opportunities and to identify ways to foster the exchange of ideas among computing and communications researchers and federal managers, including mechanisms for technology transition from the laboratory to government agencies and ultimately to operational government systems.

The first phase of the committee's work focused on two illustrative application areas—crisis management and federal statistics. In each case, the study committee convened a workshop to facilitate interaction between stakeholders from the individual domains and researchers in computing and communications systems and to explore research topics that might be of relevance throughout the government. The initial workshop in the series, held in December 1998, convened IT researchers and crisis management professionals from all levels of government and the private sector. The second workshop, held in February 1999, explored how IT research could contribute to more effective collection, processing, and dissemination of federal statistical data. This second workshop was conducted in cooperation with the National Research Council's Committee on National Statistics (CNSTAT).

The second phase of the study, culminating in the preparation of this report, combined what was learned in the two workshops with the results of previous CSTB reports and other efforts to examine IT research and e-government.[1] To supplement what was learned in the workshops, the committee held two other meetings that included data-gathering sessions. Staff and individual committee members augmented the information obtained from these meetings by interviewing government officials working on e-government initiatives. In July 2001, the committee issued a letter report to the National Science Foundation laying out the rationale

---

[1]This information included three workshop reports commissioned by the National Science Foundation's Digital Government program: Sharon Dawes, Peter Bloniarz, Kristine L. Kelly, and Patricia D. Fletcher, 1999, *Some Assembly Required: Building a Digital Government for the 21st Century*, Center for Technology in Government, State University of New York at Albany, March; Herbert Schorr and Salvatore J. Stolfo, 1997, *Towards the Digital Government of the 21st Century* (a report from the Workshop on Research and Development Opportunities in Federal Information Services), June 24; and National Center for Supercomputing Applications (NCSA), University of Illinois, 1999, *Toward Improved Geographic Information Services Within a Digital Government*, NCSA, Urbana-Champaign, Ill., June.

for involving computer science researchers in e-government work (see Appendix B in this report). In completing the second phase of the study, the committee was mindful of the increased emphasis in 2002 on critical infrastructure protection (both within and outside government) as well as a variety of initiatives to harness or develop IT capabilities for homeland defense and counterterrorism.

While a number of other reports have addressed the significant challenges in better deploying today's technologies in government, this committee's final report distinguishes itself by focusing primarily on the relationships between IT research and government IT applications. Its recommendations are intended to foster connections between IT research and e-government innovation and to help catalyze the involvement of IT researchers in defining and realizing e-government programs. The committee's findings and recommendations are presented in the "Summary and Recommendations" chapter of this report; subsequent chapters provide supporting material.

The committee appreciates the encouragement and support of Larry Brandt and Valerie Gregg of the National Science Foundation. They provided vision and a wealth of information, and they gracefully accommodated a long schedule.

The committee thanks Karen Sollins for her contributions to the early stages of the work, prior to her accepting an assignment at the National Science Foundation. She contributed valuable ideas, energy, and organizational skill.

The committee also thanks the participants in the two major workshops, as well as the many individuals who responded to its requests for briefings and discussions. The committee expresses its appreciation to Andrew A. White, director of the National Research Council's Committee on National Statistics, which cosponsored the second workshop convened for this project, for his support and assistance.

The committee also acknowledges the effective support provided by the Computer Science and Telecommunications Board and staff. In particular, the committee appreciates the valuable suggestions offered by Board members during the review process. The study was supported by several CSTB staff members, in capacities ranging from organizing committee meetings and the major workshops to assisting in researching and editing of the several reports. In particular, the committee thanks Jane Griffith, for getting the project off to an excellent start and making many substantive contributions to the effort, and Marjory Blumenthal for guidance and encouragement. David Padgham provided significant research support to this project. Finally, the committee thanks study director Jon

Eisenberg for his perseverance and professionalism in seeing the project through to completion. He provided careful facilitation of the process, and he made fundamental intellectual contributions to the product.

William L. Scherlis, *Chair*

Committee on Computing and Communications Research to Enable Better Use of Information Technology in Government

Acknowledgment of Reviewers

This report has been reviewed in draft form by individuals chosen for their diverse perspectives and technical expertise, in accordance with procedures approved by the National Research Council's Report Review Committee. The purpose of this independent review is to provide candid and critical comments that will assist the institution in making its published report as sound as possible and to ensure that the report meets institutional standards for objectivity, evidence, and responsiveness to the study charge. The review comments and draft manuscript remain confidential to protect the integrity of the deliberative process. We wish to thank the following individuals for their review of this report:

Renny DiPentima, SRA International,
Kenneth L. Kraemer, University of California at Irvine,
Bruce W. McConnell, McConnell International,
John Ousterhout, Interwoven Inc., and
Robert Sproull, Sun Microsystems Laboratories.

Although the reviewers listed above provided many constructive comments and suggestions, they were not asked to endorse the conclusions or recommendations, nor did they see the final draft of the report before its release. The review of this report was overseen by Sam Fuller, Analog Devices Inc. Appointed by the National Research Council, he was responsible for making certain that an independent examination of this report was carried out in accordance with institutional procedures and that all review comments were carefully considered. Responsibility for the final content of this report rests entirely with the authoring committee and the institution.

Contents

APPENDIXES

INFORMATION TECHNOLOGY

RESEARCH,

INNOVATION,

and

E-Government

Summary and Recommendations

In response to a request from the National Science Foundation (NSF) for advice on planning for e-government innovation programs, the Computer Science and Telecommunications Board (CSTB) convened the Committee on Computing and Communications Research to Enable Better Use of Information Technology in Government. The committee was charged with examining how information technology (IT) research can improve existing government services, operations, and interactions with citizens—as well as create new ones. The first phase of the committee's study featured workshops examining two illustrative application areas— crisis management and federal statistics—and concluded with the publication of two summary reports in 1999 and 2000.[1] The second phase of the project synthesized the results of the two workshops, information gleaned from other published work on IT research and e-government, and material obtained in the course of two data-gathering meetings and supplemental individual interviews. Preliminary results of the second phase were described in a letter report to the National Science Foundation

---

[1]Computer Science and Telecommunications Board (CSTB), National Research Council (NRC). 1999. *Summary of a Workshop on Information Technology Research for Crisis Management*. National Academy Press, Washington, D.C.; and CSTB, NRC. 2000. *Summary of a Workshop on Information Technology Research for Federal Statistics*. National Academy Press, Washington, D.C.

1

in 2001 (see Appendix B). In this "Summary and Recommendations" chapter, the committee presents the final results of its study and offers recommendations intended to foster increased and more effective collaboration between IT researchers and government agencies. Chapters 1 through 4 provide supporting discussion and analysis.

Government has done much to leverage IT to deploy e-government services, but much work remains before the vision of e-government can be fully realized (see Finding 1.1, below), whether through adoption of already-existing commercial technologies and practices (Finding 2.1) or through targeted research efforts directed at helping government and its suppliers address challenging new requirements (Finding 2.2). This report identifies research challenges related to e-government and looks at these challenges in the wider context of government IT practice and the transition of innovative information technologies from the laboratory to operational systems.

The conceptualization, design, development, testing, delivery, and support of operational government IT systems for agency end users involve an extensive "supply chain" that includes system integrators, vertical suppliers, major vendors, smaller technology companies, consultants, architects, and researchers. Government end users and IT researchers are, in some sense, at opposite ends of this supply chain and so may seem to be unlikely allies. But both in fact have a natural shared interest in innovation and in meeting future needs (Findings 3.1 and 3.2). Indeed, by working together, they can conceptualize new technology opportunities— and with lower overall risk than if they had been working independently of each other. In collaborative efforts, researchers can gain understanding of the real problems that users face, and so can reduce the risks associated with the process of selecting research problems to address. Working in a government setting also provides researchers with access to artifacts— computer systems, software, and data sets—to support experimentation and study. Government end users gain understanding of emerging technologies and of the feasibility of implementing new operational concepts. In addition, there is mutual reinforcement of the dual roles of government as a farsighted customer working with its suppliers to ensure that future mission needs can be met and as an investor in long-term research with broad socioeconomic impact (Findings 3.1 and 3.3).

The establishment of ties between IT researchers and government agencies does not mean, however, that researchers and end users should somehow short-circuit the supply chain in developing new systems, or that the government will incur risks of early adoption as a result of entering into this kind of collaboration. The consequence, rather, is *less* risk for the government—because it is better informed in doing its job of defining requirements for its interactions throughout its supply chain. Indeed, success in this overall model requires care and thought regarding technology transition at all stages of the supply chain (Findings 2.3 and 4.2).

THE OPPORTUNITIES AND CHALLENGES OF E-GOVERNMENT

Finding 1.1. Early efforts have demonstrated the potential of e-government, though much work remains before that potential can be fully realized. Achieving that potential will require addressing a broad set of interrelated issues regarding organization, policy, technology development and transition, systems architecture, and engineering practice. In addressing these issues, the government will benefit from collaboration with the computer science research community.

The emergence of the Internet and other technologies for electronic commerce has led naturally to the development of "digital government" or "e-government" services—the application of information technology, combined with changes in agency practices, to develop more responsive, efficient, and accountable government operations. During the 1990s, federal legislative and executive branch initiatives and state and local government efforts added impetus, fostering experimentation and new programs. Early government Web sites were the pioneering creations of enterprising individuals and groups. Today government agency and organization Web sites get attention from the highest levels of government and the most senior officials. Underscoring the importance of government IT capability, in 2002 the federal government appointed a chief technology officer, whose mission includes coordination of efforts in e-government. E-government—which has diverse constituencies that include citizens and other individuals; businesses; nonprofit organizations; and the many federal, state, and local agencies—is envisioned as providing some of the following key benefits:

- More accessible government information;
- Faster, smoother transactions with government agencies;
- Enhanced ubiquity of access to information and transactions;
- Greater effectiveness in meeting the needs of specific groups of users;
- Increased participation in government by all people, fostering a more informed and engaged citizenry;
- Greater ability to meet expectations for advances in government-unique areas, including challenges in the newly emerging homeland security mission; and
- More efficient internal government operations.

Ideas from early experiments in e-government have contributed both to technology development and to the improvement of government practices. A tremendous amount of experience already exists in creating and deploying e-government capabilities. This experience resides in state and local government as well as in a broad span of federal agencies. Increasingly, the best practices emerging from this experience are being adopted by many government agencies.

From the citizen's perspective, among the most visible enhancements have been new means for the public to access government information, the development of task-oriented cross-agency portals (such as seniors. gov and students.gov), and the recently launched governmentwide portal firstgov.gov. Other visible illustrations include computer-based tax filing and inquiry-response services that are provided by multiple agencies, each accessed through a task-oriented Web portal.

The benefits to business have also been considerable, including broader access to government data, more rapid and efficient interaction with regulatory agencies (such as electronic filing of diverse required reports and comments on proposed regulations), and streamlined acquisition and procurement processes. In addition, administrative burdens associated with initiating and managing small and start-up businesses are being reduced through online resources.

Much work remains if government is to fully realize the ambition of broadening e-government services from information access to transaction support—services that enable citizens, businesses, and other government entities to submit information to, engage in financial transactions with, or otherwise interact with government organizations. Much also remains to be done in enhancing systems used for information management and collaboration among government officials and agencies. In these realms, issues such as confidentiality, data integrity, information management, and usability can present significant obstacles. These issues mix technology and policy, and they can be difficult to address without appropriate collaboration between the technology and policy communities.

Also apparent—from briefings and workshops organized by this committee and in news accounts from across the country—are difficulties experienced by government agencies seeking to deploy new capabilities. The committee identified a number of challenges to the government's effective exploitation of IT. These challenges, which encompass a mix of research and implementation issues, include the following:

- Ensuring the interoperation and integration of diverse systems used by different departments and agencies with multiple stakeholders and a significant legacy base;
- Adapting organizational structures so as to maximize their effec-

tiveness in concert with IT-based innovation, which tends to be harder in government than in the private sector;

- Improving trustworthiness, including guarantees of information-systems security as well as assurances regarding user privacy and system availability;
- Bridging significant gaps between current practices and best-available practices; and
- Meeting specific technology needs related to government missions.

Recommendation 1.1. Government should continue to improve its support for transactions with individuals, businesses, and organizations. In doing so, it should emulate, where possible, the commercial trend toward integration of services to improve usability for customers. This means, for example, that government should continue the transition from program- or agency-centered service offerings to user-centered services, which can imply aggregating services from multiple government agencies and potentially from private-sector third parties.

A number of major government online services display a mature realization of information-access technology. Future steps are likely to be much more technically challenging. For example, functionality will expand from emphasizing information access to providing comprehensive support for the multitude of transactions between government and users (citizens, businesses, and other organizations), which significantly lags information access today. Correspondingly, modalities will expand beyond people's interacting with Web browsers to include routine online access to government information and services through common programming interfaces and access through devices other than desktop computers. As these services evolve, governments will have to figure out how best to leverage IT as part of overall customer service strategies. Part of the process has been adopting a customer service perspective on interactions with citizens, businesses, and others—a trend that began even before the widespread use of the Internet.

To better meet customer needs and serve particular customer groups, such as small businesses or students, businesses are participating in the rapid coevolution of e-business technology and commercial processes. Today, improvement in customer focus is often accomplished by reorganizing corporate structure to aggregate information and transaction services in ways that better serve specific market segments. Although the process can be organizationally difficult and technically challenging, business organizations have often been able to reorganize internally to match the procedural flows appropriate to the new "portal" technologies—for example, by restructuring to bypass intermediaries in relationships. Government has been taking some initial steps in this direction as well, as evidenced by multiple government-information portals (firstgov.gov, fedstats.gov, seniors.gov, and others) that aggregate information from individual agency Web sites and early efforts to aggregate transaction services from multiple agencies. In deciding whether to provide integrated capabilities, an organization must weigh the potential benefits against the technical challenges. Integration is hard and the results tend to be fragile (a change in one of the systems being integrated may cause cascading effects).

As alluded to above, one complication special to the government setting is that integration is fraught with legal and structural challenges. Legal constraints can significantly inhibit rapid, wholesale structural changes in government structures (at both inter- and intraagency levels). For example, legal and regulatory barriers to sharing information have been established to protect citizen privacy. At the same time, the stovepiped appropriations process—in which agencies compete for resources and appropriations that are determined by separate congressional committees—makes cross-agency collaboration to build more integrated systems very difficult. Explicit authorization and resources to undertake cross-agency efforts is an important element of a solution. Also, as noted above, governments differ from businesses in their inherently comprehensive scope. Finally, the desired span of aggregation can include state and local governments as well as federal agencies.

One option for building integrated user-oriented services is the use of intermediary software that draws on data from multiple sources to formulate a set of smaller queries that can be separately dispatched to databases operated by different government entities. For example, an augmentation to fedstats.gov could be devised to support an increasing range of aggregate queries that combine statistical data held by individual agencies.

Intermediaries might be operated commercially as well as by government. Indeed, a competitive market of commercial services that conduct transactions with multiple separate agencies could result in improved access to government services, suggesting that government should explore this opportunity. For example, a commercial service might interact with government transaction services to undertake all of the actions required to register a new small business. An interesting challenge with respect to commercial services is how to provide the expected level of confidentiality and integrity of information, especially as the point of aggregation shifts from government to third parties. Meeting this challenge will require codevelopment of both policy and technical safeguards. For example, some of the data that government collects from individuals is subject to legislative or regulatory safeguards designed to keep anyone but the individual from combining the information.

At present, much of the thinking about e-government focuses on what can be delivered with today's technology; this is reflected in the foregoing finding and recommendation. But it is also essential that, in looking ahead, planners contemplate how both technology and user expectations will evolve. This is another element of the rationale for direct collaboration and interaction between technology innovators and end users.

GOVERNMENT INFORMATION TECHNOLOGY PRACTICE

The delivery of new digital government services depends on access to advanced information technology, the right management strategies and processes within organizations adopting the new technology, and effective, ongoing evaluation of new service concepts and goals.

Technologies and Practices

Finding 2.1. Many aspects of e-government development can and should follow the marketplace in selecting technology and associated practices.

Recommendation 2.1. Government should adopt commercial e-commerce technologies and associated practices wherever possible.

Government can make considerable progress toward the e-government vision even without new research results. Businesses (and government) have made significant strides as they have made use of rapidly maturing Internet-based information technologies and responded to the corresponding growth in user expectations. Because the technologies and processes that underlie digital services in government are in most respects similar to those used in e-business, government obviously benefits when it can exploit off-the-shelf components, infrastructure, systems, and successful practices already used in the private sector. In many cases, government can and should follow the example of business with respect to service concepts, technical standards, infrastructural components, and interface design. Recognition of this point is reflected in more than a decade of movement toward increasing use of commercial off-the-shelf technology for government applications. (Of course, for some specific applications and systems, there may be no off-the-shelf option.)

When government systems exploit widely used standards and technologies, government can "ride the curves" of performance growth and enhancement that are characteristic of the broader IT marketplace. Program managers must balance these benefits in cost and capability with the added uncertainty that they can experience in the management of systems whose evolution is less under their control compared to that of systems custom-built for specific purposes.

Finding 2.2. Although government should maximize the use of commercial technology as it builds e-government capabilities, government requirements sometimes differ from those found in the commercial world. With respect to requirements for such capabilities as ubiquity (and others listed below), government is a "demand leader." Targeted research in computer science, coupled with effective technology transition strategies, can contribute significantly to the development of such capabilities.

Although it can generally build on the technologies and services emerging in the e-business marketplace, government leads demand in several areas. Research in these areas can help government agencies better accomplish their missions and also—with the right research-management strategies—stimulate commercial interest and development. Successful stimulation of the commercial marketplace could enable government to move more rapidly away from acquisition of expensive custom systems, whose full life-cycle costs government must bear, to the use of less costly off-the-shelf commercial capabilities. As the result of such investments in the past, government now can make use, for example, of commercial operating systems with enhanced security (e.g., better process separation), multimedia databases, and packet-switched networking equipment. In the experience of mission agencies such as the U.S. Department of Defense (DOD), National Aeronautics and Space Administration (NASA), and U.S. Department of Energy (DOE), this strategy has been effective not only in areas where government leads demand, but also in areas where aggressive requirements for innovation are shared by government and the commercial sector.

Important areas of leading demand (discussed in more detail in the main text of this report) include these:

• *Ubiquity.* Governments must provide services to all citizens—they cannot, in general, opt to serve only the easiest-to-reach customers or participate only in particular market segments. Nor can citizens choose which government they will deal with. The breadth of service provided by government must encompass a wide range of individuals' physical, cognitive, and language abilities as well as their education, income, and geographic location. Near-universal communications access is provided today primarily through telephone and postal mail interactions, but e-mail, the World Wide Web, public information kiosks, and other IT-based approaches are providing new opportunities to expand the range and accessibility of services. Research in areas such as human-computer interaction, information retrieval, language translation, and speech recognition and synthesis can help increase the ubiquity of such services. Achieving usability and accessibility requires that systems be evaluated in realistic settings, and government applications may provide a range of contexts in which researchers can frame their efforts.

• *Trustworthiness.* Citizens expect government to provide assurances of security—including confidentiality (protection of personal and business information), integrity of information and systems, and availability of information and systems—that are generally stronger than those expected of the private sector. But what is expected or desired may be beyond what technology and practice can actually offer. Conventional business practice incorporates risk management, in which the costs of implementing security measures are balanced against the consequences of not having them, and these calculations sometimes show that certain levels of exposure can be tolerated for certain applications. (Credit card fraud is an example.) Government agencies, however, are expected to adhere to a higher standard—no improper disclosure of personal information contained in statistical data, tax filings, social security records, and the like—even though government is also charged with releasing certain kinds of information, which may be derived from sensitive personal or corporate information that it collects, and making it uniformly available to all.

Trust in public systems is essential for citizens' compliance with government mandates (e.g., paying taxes, completing census forms); equally critical is trust in the safety and reliability of systems on which people's lives may depend. In military applications, requirements for trustworthiness have led to efforts to promote "high-assurance" technologies for critical systems; similar requirements apply to IT in the transportation and health arenas, in which government is often in partnership with the private sector. In the wake of the September 11, 2001, attacks, there is increased attention to protection of critical infrastructure, including both government and private sector infrastructure. Addressing issues related to trustworthiness involves intermingled considerations of policy, organizational behavior and culture, and technology. Computer science research can contribute tools and approaches for facilitating dissemination of information without compromising confidentiality, as well as for designing and developing systems that provide appropriate, comparatively high overall levels of trustworthiness (as is the intent of the federal interagency High Confidence Software and Systems research program).

• *Information heterogeneity and semantic interoperability.* Like other large entities, governments confront significant organizational and technical challenges when they seek to use information drawn from multiple sources. Integration is especially difficult in ad hoc situations—such as when federal, state, and local agencies must establish an "instant bureaucracy" to respond to a crisis and support recovery efforts. But integration is difficult in preplanned situations as well—such as when agencies seek to serve customers through aggregation of services (see next bulleted item) or to share information in order to comply with legislative or administrative directives (e.g., mandates to exchange state welfare data or to monitor visa status and U.S. border crossings). Because agency information systems are generally "stovepiped"—that is, they employ different and often incompatible conventions for data format and semantics—such information sharing and data fusion can be difficult. (On the other hand, there can be privacy risks when fusion can be easily accomplished, as is discussed in Chapter 2, in the subsection "Access and Confidentiality.") Organizational barriers, including a frequent reluctance to share information across agency boundaries, further complicate matters. Technological responses include efforts to employ prevailing commercial standards, develop common standards, and develop improved capabilities to translate information across systems.

• *Providing software interfaces to services.* The provision of application-programming interfaces (APIs) or structured data representations (as in use of the markup language XML) can enable third parties to engage government services on behalf of clients. The Internal Revenue Service (IRS), for example, now allows commercial tax-preparation firms to file returns electronically. Health care researchers, as another example, are actively creating XML representations in order to more readily exchange, combine, and analyze clinical trial data. More generally, appropriate interfaces would also enable citizens and businesses to use software that directly connects with government services. A number of technical challenges exist, though, including protocol design, development of information representations and metadata standards, security and authentication, and development of digital library systems. Government has historically provided data in electronic form, but often the design of the formats makes it infeasible for all but a few specialized contractors to exploit the data readily. Achieving "lightweight" protocols or standards can be difficult, however, because of the often-large number of specific cases that must be handled—for example, those relating to seemingly simple data items such as names and addresses.

• *Building large-scale systems.* Many problems associated with large-scale systems—including delays, unexpected failures, and inflexibility in coping with changing needs—exist in government at all levels. Budgetary constraints also dictate the development of systems that can be sustained at low cost. Continued research activity, involving case studies of particular systems as well as methodology research on architecture, techniques, and tools, is needed to address the difficult challenges, technical and nontechnical, posed in realizing these systems.

Finding 2.3. In building e-government systems and the supporting digital infrastructure, government faces significant nontechnical challenges in the way it acquires IT capabilities.

Best practices in government acquisition already recognize the iterative nature of systems development, due to the simultaneous evolution of technology capability, user requirements, and the environment in which a system is used. For example, the Information Technology Management Reform Act of 1996 (the Clinger-Cohen Act) promotes iterative processes in mainstream IT systems acquisition. Contracts with system integrators that were built around a traditional waterfall acquisition model—in which one first defines the full set of requirements for a system and then builds a system that complies with those specifications—are widely understood to be inadequate except for systems whose requirements are well understood at the outset, and for which there is a corresponding base of experience in design and operation. A characteristic of iterative processes is that life-cycle requirements and/or the engineering design space may not be fully understood at the outset. Iterative processes are also appropriate when unexpected changes in the operating environment are likely.

In electronic business, the frequency of iteration can be very rapid, with consequently high demand on capability for acquisition and engineering management. This fast pace of e-business evolution is shaping expectations for the delivery of government services, creating pressure for an even more rapid pace of evolution in capability and scope. This places even greater demand on government's ability to manage its relationships with its technology supply chain, including system integrators, vertical suppliers, vendors, start-up technology companies, and researchers. For IT systems, a particular challenge is that there are rapid changes both in underlying technologies and in the expectations of customers. Users seek to avoid getting locked in to rapidly obsolescing technologies and practices—which implies that nontechnical, market-based decision criteria can be significant. Incentives that promote risk sharing between vendors and the government in the development of innovative solutions are also helpful. Complicating the situation is the persistent challenge faced by government in attracting, retaining, and rewarding program managers who can effectively articulate and negotiate the government's long-term interests in contracts with system integrators and other vendors.

WHY E-GOVERNMENT RESEARCH?

Sustaining the IT Technical Base and Addressing Government Needs

> **Finding 3.1. By leveraging its dual roles as a user of IT and a long-term investor in IT research, government can increase its awareness of the opportunities afforded by IT advances and influence the development of IT that can help to meet its own needs. This synergy can be stimulated by government through investment throughout the technology supply chain and through the development of relationships with all appropriate segments of the IT research, development, and vendor communities.**

Like all major IT customers, government has an interest in the management of its future, which includes maintaining both awareness and influence throughout its IT supply chain. This suggests that there is value for government in developing relationships with diverse segments of the IT research, development, vendor, consultant, and integrator communities.

Government has an additional role, however, as a long-term, patient investor in IT research, particularly with respect to research results that have broad value (Finding 3.4). In this role, the government creates public goods with broad and significant socioeconomic value—such as new algorithms, conventions enabling interoperation, measurement methods, shared testbeds, and the like.

> **Finding 3.2. A cooperative alliance between researchers and agency end users in defining requirements for new IT-based capabilities has benefits for both groups. Researchers gain a better understanding of the real challenges and obstacles, along with access to data and artifacts that can inform or validate design. Agency users, especially those that lack in-house research capability, gain understanding of emerging and future technologies. By collaborating directly, the two groups can more rapidly converge on requirements that meet real needs and that are technologically achievable—and that may not have been expected by either party in advance of the collaboration.**

Interaction between researchers and end users on problems of mutual interest has become increasingly important to progress in many areas of IT. Working on government IT problems in particular offers researchers a number of potential benefits—an important one being access both to subject-matter experts and to associated artifacts that are needed in computer science research. A government setting gives researchers access to applications with a richness and texture typically lacking in the laboratory, and it may also provide a less constrained environment as it is less subject to proprietary considerations that are often associated with work in the private sector. The National Science Foundation's Digital Government program, which funds collaborative research between computer science researchers and government agencies, has begun to demonstrate the potential of such collaborations.

For government agencies, benefits stemming from research can extend well beyond the research results themselves. While there is no substitute for in-house IT talent, interactions with researchers are a useful way to tap additional technical expertise, especially top-caliber research talent that is unlikely to be obtainable in-house or through the usual advisory mechanisms. In addition, sustained involvement by a research community in a mission area helps define the metaphors and problems that drive that community. This is evident among researchers who have worked over long periods with DOD, DOE, and NASA, for example. Some of the most significant benefits of government mission research investment can be indirect, because research results can have considerable value beyond the particular application area and because research on hard and long-term problems sometimes leads to unanticipated breakthroughs. Although it is very difficult to do a precise evaluation, these additional indirect benefits have to be considered when assessing the ultimate impact and value of government research programs. Finally, a close collaboration between researchers and agency users can create an environment for stimulating creative solutions to challenges, for example, through rapid iteration of prototypes. (See Chapter 4, "Technology Transition and Program Management: Bridging the Gap Between Research and Impact.")

Finding 3.3. A sound foundation for e-government and other applications of information technology throughout society depends on a continuing, broad, federal computer science research program.

The historical record shows that broad and sustained federal investment in IT research has nurtured the development of computer technology and the IT industry. Many IT research programs not only reached their intended goals, whether mission or scientific, but also stimulated commercial products, companies, and indeed industries. They also contributed fundamentally to the training of researchers and practitioners, who often transferred technologies to the commercial sector through employment or entrepreneurship. Illustrations can be found, for example, in distributed transaction processing, raster displays, very-large-scale integrated circuit design, and data mining.

Indeed, the rapid rise of e-business in the 1990s—and subsequent e-government development—was based on a variety of information technologies that were developed incrementally over a period of many decades, eventually reaching a point of maturity, scale, and usability that allowed them to be incorporated directly into the infrastructures of commerce and government. The rapid growth in the past decade was also based on the acceptance of an evolving set of common standards that enabled scaling up, competition, and interoperation. The development of the Internet suite of protocols, along with the establishment of processes for evolving them, is perhaps the most widely recognized example. A significant portion of these technologies and standards resulted directly from ongoing, farsighted government investment by a number of research agencies. Indeed, without this investment, it could be argued that the Internet phenomenon would not have come into existence—it was by no means an inevitable development.

When mission goals are approached strategically, new thinking can be infused into a mission agency's supply chain of vendors and technology developers, which can yield major dividends for government. For example, products or standards that address government needs can be acquired off the shelf rather than by developing more expensive custom systems. Of course, these products or standards might have emerged without government investment, but quite possibly at the cost of considerable delay.

> **Finding 3.4. In areas of research whose benefits cannot be fully retained by the investor—areas in which the private sector may not be able to justify investment—government investment can be critical to creating new technology capabilities and opportunities for all participants, including government itself.**

Universities and some private sector research laboratories have long led in the development of the core technical underpinnings of e-business, in the education of the IT workforce, and in many aspects of the creation of new technologies and technological commonalities. Building in part on past research results, the U.S. information technology industries have seen tremendous growth. Even with this growth and success, government investment—both from research and mission agencies—in IT research and education continues to enhance the overall competitive position of the U.S. information technology industry. The government role in addressing long-term issues continues to be unique and critical.

This special role of government in IT research investment can be understood in the light of typical industry return-on-investment calculations—which generally (but not always) preclude innovations that are fundamentally long term in character or that have broad and nonspecific impact. In the language of economics, many of these innovations are nonappropriable—the results of the research diffuse broadly into the technical community and cannot successfully be retained by a single sponsoring organization for its exclusive use. Similarly, particular innovations may be competition-neutral or their impacts may be unpredictable; such innovations, though they could be of broad benefit across the industry, are therefore not in a company's self-interest to support. (See the discussion of nonappropriability in the subsection "Will Industry Do It?" in Chapter 4.)

Among the products of such research innovation in diverse technical areas are Internet protocol standards, algorithm-analysis techniques, programming-language foundations, and, to a great extent, technologies for interoperation. Government investments leading to such broad benefits not only serve the sponsoring agencies' needs but also have much wider impact by creating new technologies that can be used by all participants, public and private.

Finding 3.5. There are a number of broad technical areas where government investment in IT research would be particularly likely to have an impact on the creation of more advanced capabilities in e-government.

Enhancements to a number of classes of technologies would greatly facilitate the building of advanced e-government capabilities. These include, for example:

- *Information infrastructure and e-commerce technologies,* which provide the foundation for e-business outside and inside government;
- *Information management technologies,* which permit search and retrieval from the very large volumes of information held by governments and allow integration of diverse sets of heterogeneous information systems;
- *Middleware,* which provides common services and capabilities that "glue" software components together into larger systems;
- *Human-system interfaces,* which provide "every-citizen" usability;
- *Modeling and simulation,* which are important tools underlying government planning and decision making (such as in crisis management); and
- *Software technologies,* which permit construction of more robust, larger-scale, interdependent software systems.

Details of each research area are provided in Chapter 3 of this report.

Recommendation 3.1. The federal government should continue to participate actively in developing a full range of information technologies. At the same time, government should leverage its role as a long-term supporter of IT research to embrace e-government challenges within its broad research programs and to stimulate more targeted technology development to meet particular needs.

E-government research encompasses targeted research to meet particular mission needs, research in technical areas where government leads in demand (Finding 2.2), and broad research of benefit to e-government and elsewhere (Finding 3.5). In each case, government research programs can take steps to stimulate a broader commercial response as well as meet government needs. A historical example of this kind of government stimulus is the development of distribution and security support for operating systems. To meet the demand for large-scale and reliable distributed computing in the Department of Defense, the government invested over a period of many years in underlying technical approaches and engineering-process concepts. The resulting technologies not only address specific government needs but also have formed the basis of mainstream commercial systems.

STIMULATING INFORMATION TECHNOLOGY INNOVATION AND TRANSITION INTO OPERATIONAL SYSTEMS

Within the federal government, some mission agencies—including DOD, NASA, DOE, the National Institutes of Health (NIH), and the Environmental Protection Agency (EPA)—maintain research capability that supports both intra- and extramural research in innovative IT. Government also has a number of mission areas, such as federal statistics and crisis management, that are supported by multiple entities and for which explicit coordination mechanisms have been devised (such as the cooperation between federal statistical agencies and the Office of Management and Budget [OMB], the lead role played by the Federal Emergency Management Agency [FEMA] among federal agencies in crisis management, or the emerging coordination potential of the new Office of Homeland Security). In addition, mechanisms within government coordinate research and development activity in certain key technology areas such as geographic information systems and high-performance computing. Government is taking action to ensure that its long-term needs are addressed in these areas of shared mission, shared reliance on aggressive technology, or both.

The sections above considered basic research and exploratory development that contribute to understanding of core concepts and key design issues. The next subsections consider additional success factors in this innovation process.

Stimulating Innovation in Systems Building

Finding 4.1. Most government agencies have limited capability (or mandates) to manage IT research programs or to undertake exploratory IT development or aggressive prototyping programs. While some agencies would benefit from developing this capability, for others it may be more effective, with respect to cost and risk, to collaborate with agencies facing similar challenges.

To address their technological needs, most federal, state, and local agencies must choose between acquiring off-the-shelf products and building custom systems. In the former case, costs may be low, but the agency customer has less control over product capability and can exert influence on vendor product plans only in proportion to its (relatively small) share of the market. In the latter case, the agency customer defines the capability but must also bear the total costs of ownership over the lifetime of the system, including explicit management of system evolution and interoperation.

Recommendation 4.1. Consideration should be given to providing specific mechanisms, such as a centrally managed cross-agency IT innovation fund, as incentives to enable government organizations to undertake innovative and risky IT projects.

Agencies, particularly in their acquisition activities, may need explicit incentives and process models in order to stimulate and exploit leading-edge technologies. In many cases, early digital-government capability emerged primarily as a result of imaginative, independently entrepreneurial federal employees taking initiative and accepting risks, but this approach does not scale. Agencies are normally driven by prudence to make conservative decisions in setting requirements and establishing incentives for contractors to deliver within cost and schedule constraints. A centrally managed innovation fund can provide funding resources that help "buy down the risk" for a would-be innovator and a group of experts who can work with contractors to help them develop innovative solutions. Such a fund can also provide opportunities for sharing best practices, experimental integration, scaling up of prototypes, and creation of evaluation testbeds. NSF's Digital Government grant-making program has demonstrated the concept on a small scale.

Building the Bridge Between Research, Systems Development, and Government Innovation

Finding 4.2. Success in the development of innovative systems depends not only on underlying technical capability but also on research-management strategy. In particular, the transition of new technologies into operational systems remains one of the areas of greatest risk and difficulty.

Even assuming that there are sufficient incentives and rewards for innovation in IT development, huge challenges remain in moving new technology into government operations—from research to prototype development and operational experimentation. This "middle" set of technology development stages is central to successful realization of the vision of digital government, and it can be the most problematic and least controllable portion of the overall process of innovation. There is more to the story than simply understanding the tensions between the risk-averse, operationally focused culture of the acquisition system and the risk-tolerant, future-focused culture of the IT research community.

In particular, managing this set of transitional stages can mean working across the entire supply chain of IT innovation, recognizing that each of the participants—government system integrators, vertical application developers, vendors of major components such as databases and operating systems, technology-focused start-up companies, and university and laboratory researchers, among others—has its own unique set of incentives and interests.

One of the greatest challenges is how to escape from the "specification-first" acquisition model, which one sees even in some prototyping programs that were meant to be exploratory and to undertake risks. Effective innovation in systems development requires simultaneous commitment to developing new technology and to defining new concepts of operation. In this model, iteration (in the sense of the spiral model from software engineering, in which a sequence of prototypes of increasing functionality is created) is undertaken both with respect to definition of operational concept and development of the technology. Ironically, adoption of the spiral model may increase overall programmatic risk (for development projects) unless it is carefully managed—which is one reason that sequential models are often adopted even when incentives exist to use iterative approaches.

Regardless, exploratory IT development and prototyping programs are an important mechanism for better exploiting new IT. Such applied research allows agencies to evaluate potential new capabilities and to assess their implications for operational concepts.

Recommendation 4.2. The federal government should develop more effective means for undertaking multiagency collaborative efforts that support aggressive prototyping, technology evaluation, and technology transition in support of e-government.

The recent emphasis in government on homeland security, including the development of new science and technology in support of the counterterrorism mission, has fostered new attention to cross-agency activities related to information technology. The appointment during the Bush administration of a federal chief technology officer and development of an associate director for information technology and e-government within OMB reinforces both the need and the potential for crosscutting activity. Circumstances have become more propitious than expected at the outset of this study for the kind of cross-agency program development that the committee believes is required and appropriate.

Government agencies that lack robust in-house IT research capabilities should explore research partnerships with agencies that do have them. Several agencies currently manage IT research programs that aim both to conduct IT research in support of agency mission requirements and to stimulate IT innovation more broadly. These agencies include NSF, the Defense Advanced Research Projects Agency (DARPA), DOE, and NASA, as well as the National Institute of Standards and Technology (which is charged with addressing measurement, standards, and interoperability challenges). Each of these agencies has in-house capabilities, an IT research culture, and existing relationships with the IT research community that could prove useful in e-government innovation programs. NSF has already established research partnerships on a modest scale through its Digital Government program, which could be expanded to include more government partners. Others might also explore development of such programs where there is a natural alignment of existing missions with common requirements. Given these various options for supporting e-government-related research, it would appear more appropriate for agencies lacking in-house IT capabilities to tap some combination of these existing capabilities (possibly adding some coordination mechanisms) than to create a new entity to manage e-government research.

Recommendation 4.3. To ensure success in the development and transition of new technologies, explicit attention should be given to program-management practices. Research program managers should be cognizant of the complexities of technology development and transition processes, and aware, in particular, of the range of program-management models and strategies that could be employed.

By facilitating collaboration among mission agencies and government research organizations, it may be possible to address areas of shared concern, such as security, more effectively. Cross-agency attention is evident in OMB, the federal Chief Information Officers Council, and in congressional activity, but it has only infrequently translated into long-lived relationships being established to do research or to undertake prototyping studies. Details of various program-management strategies are provided in Chapter 4 of this report.

1

Vision for IT-Enabled Enhancement of Government

Government expenditures on information technology (IT) are substantial. In Fiscal Year 2001, the total annual federal IT investment was roughly $44.5 billion.[1] This level of spending reflects government's great reliance on IT systems in carrying out its diverse missions. The emergence of the Internet into the mainstream, along with the growth of other electronic-commerce technologies, is fundamentally altering the environment in which government delivers services to citizens, businesses, and other government entities. These innovations in technology and business practices have given rise to the concept of "e-government," which refers to the adoption of electronic-business practices in government.

Estimates of the fraction of this spending that goes toward e-government vary, depending on what criteria are used to distinguish e-government initiatives from other IT programs. The consulting firm Gartner Group recently estimated that federal, state, and local spending on government-to-government, government-to-business, and government-to-citizen initiatives was roughly $1.5 billion in 2000 (with the projection that this sum will grow to more than $6.2 billion in 2005),[2] while the

---

[1]Office of Management and Budget (OMB). 2001. "Clinger-Cohen Act Report on Federal Information Technology Investments." OMB, Executive Office of the President, Washington, D.C., April 9. Available online at <http://www.whitehouse.gov/omb/inforeg/final53.xls>.

[2]Gartner Group. 2000. "Gartner Says U.S. E-Government Spending to Surpass $6.2 Billion by 2005" (press release), April 11. Available online at <http://gartner11.gartnerweb.com/public/static/aboutgg/pressrel/pr041100c.html>.

market research company Input estimated the current expenditures at about $7.2 billion.[3]

At the same time that government is seeking to apply IT in new ways to fulfill its own particular obligations, the role of government with respect to broad-based IT development and use is also shifting. In recent decades, the private sector has surpassed government leadership in many areas of IT adoption and use, even as government continues to play a critical—some would say increasingly critical—role as a principal agent for long-term IT basic research and innovation.

Much like their counterparts in the private sector, many in government are actively experimenting with the harnessing of new Internet and other information technologies to improve operations and the delivery of services. A wide range of ideas is emerging from these experiments, contributing to technology development, the improvement of business practices, a more streamlined government, and a more sophisticated public. Traditionally, formal paper-based information dissemination was undertaken by specialized document-distribution services such as the Government Printing Office and the National Technical Information Service. With the rise of the World Wide Web, agency-specific sites that provide access to a range of documents and databases have been developed over the past several years. Complementing the development of Web sites available through the Internet, agencies such as the U.S. Department of Housing and Urban Development (HUD), the General Services Administration (GSA), and the Office of Personnel Management (OPM) have also developed kiosk systems, using Web technology, to provide access to information resources in public locations.

The federal government now offers a number of information portals, which aggregate and present government information for access by customers in particular "market segments" (such as students, workers, or senior citizens) and provide links to commonly performed transactions. In 2000, a federal governmentwide portal, firstgov.gov, which provides a search engine across federal Web sites along with a directory of commonly used sites and services, was launched;[4] a number of other, more targeted, federal portals also exist (see Box 1.1).

With these efforts, a rapidly increasing corpus of government-gener-

---

[3]William Mathews. 2000. "E-gov Leads IT Spending Forecast." *Federal Computer Week*, December 8. Available online at <http://www.fcw.com/fcw/articles/2000/1204/web-egov-12-08-00.asp>.

[4]Generally hailed as a promising next step, the Web site is not without controversy. Concerns include the management structure and relationship between the private foundation responsible for the search engine component and whether the search engine returns the most relevant, useful results.

ated information is available directly to users via the Internet, and IT is being exploited to deliver government services in new ways, including the use of the Internet to conduct transactions that previously required postal mail or an in-person visit.

Indeed, various agencies and programs were early adopters of Web technology, and some level of online presence, albeit with varying degrees of sophistication, is the norm for government today at the federal and state levels. At the same time, inputs received by the Committee on Computing and Communications Research to Enable Better Use of Information Technology in Government, over the course of two workshops and during additional discussions with informed individuals, suggest that the federal government generally continues to lag behind the private sector both in adopting present-day technology and in addressing its own special needs. The committee's in-depth examinations of two areas—federal statistics and crisis management—suggest that while a good deal of experimentation is occurring and considerable experience is being gained in implementing a range of sophisticated capabilities, many systems significantly lag behind the state of the art. For example, the committee's consideration of the federal statistical agencies revealed that while fedstats.gov, coordinated by the Federal Interagency Council on Statistical Policy, was of one of the earliest implementations of interagency portals, there was also an instance in which the Bureau of the Census had only recently retired an obsolete Univac computer system. The inquires of the committee also revealed cases of government bodies having very specific technology needs that have not been adequately addressed. These include, for example, software to support the complex surveys administered by the federal statistical agencies and a number of crisis- and consequence-management applications.

According to a recent report from the National Association of State Information Resource Executives, many states have also made the transition from presenting a simple directory of agencies to a portal design in which available information is organized around the needs of specific user segments. Several states planned to develop portals in partnership with an outside vendor, with an expectation that the vendor would be compensated through transaction fees.[5] A number of these portals represent a fairly mature realization of present-day information-access technology, but considerable scope for improvement remains. Box 1.2 provides several examples of state e-government services.

---

[5]National Association of State Information Resource Executives (NASIRE). 2000. *Preliminary Survey of the Digital Government Landscape*. NASIRE, Lexington, Kentucky. Available online at <http://www.nasire.org/publications/digital_government_report_2000.pdf>.

Box 1.1
Examples of Federal Government Information Portals

• *FirstGov* <www.firstgov.gov>. The portal FirstGov was established as a joint project of the federal government and the private FedSearch Foundation, which oversees the site's search engine. Funded in 2001 and 2002 from the General Services Administration (GSA) and 22 federal agencies, FirstGov is managed by GSA's Office of FirstGov.[1] The Web site provides a search engine that uses an index of Web pages government wide as well as a directory of commonly accessed information resources and services.

• *Access America for Seniors* <www.seniors.gov>. A government information portal dedicated to the needs of seniors, Access America for Seniors exemplifies a site that attempts to make the resources of multiple agencies available to a particular user group. It was developed through the cooperation of the National Partnership for Reinventing Government (NPR) and several other interested organizations, including the Social Security Administration, the Administration on Aging, the U.S. Department of Housing and Urban Development, the U.S. Department of Veterans Affairs, and the American Association of Retired Persons.

• *Access America for Students* <www.students.gov>. As with Access America for Seniors, Access America for Students was created to serve a specialized group of users. Developed and maintained through the cooperation of NPR and the U.S. Department of Education, the site offers links to information about planning an education, financial aid, career development, community service, travel, military service, and more. It also contains an array of links to legislative, executive, and judicial Web sites.

• *FedStats* <www.fedstats.gov>. FedStats is maintained by the Federal Interagency Council on Statistical Policy to provide users with easy access to the full range of statistics and information produced by more than 70 participating government agencies.[2] Funding is provided by in-kind donations of services and small contributions from 12 federal statistical agencies to support hardware and software procurement and dedicated manpower. Participating agencies host their own statistics on their own servers; FedStats provides an efficient gateway to their information. For instance, if one selects the Crime link in the subject index, FedStats forwards the user to the U.S. Department of Justice's Bureau of Justice Statistics Web Site. Also, FedStats contains a feature called MapStats, through which users can locate statistical information about particular U.S. states or counties by clicking on a series of maps.

• *U.S. Consumer Gateway* <www.consumer.gov>. U.S. Consumer Gateway was created by the Federal Trade Commission (FTC), and the FTC continues to maintain it with the participation of the Securities and Exchange Commission, the Consumer Product Safety Commission, the Food and Drug Administration, the National Highway Traffic Safety Administration, the Environmental Protection Agency, the U.S. Department of Agriculture, the U.S. Department of the Treasury, the Federal Communications Commission, and the Federal Deposit Insurance Corporation. The

---

[1] For more on the history, funding, and management of Firstgov, see <http://www.firstgov.gov/About.shtml>.

[2] See <http://www.fedstats.gov/agencies> for a full list of participating agencies.

site is designed so that users can locate government consumer-related information by category (Food, Health, Product Safety, Money, Transportation, and so forth). Each category has further subcategories to direct users to areas within individual federal Web sites containing related information. For instance, the Product Safety category includes links to product information from the Consumer Product Safety Commission, the National Highway Traffic Safety Administration, the Food and Drug Administration, and the FTC, among others.

- *Code Talk <www.codetalk.fed.us>.* Code Talk is a federal interagency Native American Web site that provides access to a wide range of information for Native American communities. It is hosted by the Office of Native American Programs of the U.S. Department of Housing and Urban Development. Code Talk contains sections concerning "current issues" and "key topics" among Native Americans, and major subject areas include housing, health, the arts, children, and the environment. Within these broad areas, users will find links to relevant government agencies and programs. Selecting the link to environmental information, for instance, takes users to the major source of government information on this topic—the American Indian Environmental Office (<http://www.epa.gov/indian>) of the U.S. Environmental Protection Agency (EPA). The site also contains links to a host of other federal Web sites (e.g., the Bureau of Indian Affairs, the Indian Health Service, the Senate and the House of Representatives, the Government Accounting Office, and the Office of Management and Budget) and provides links to other resources and tools, including information on training and employment, laws, and taxes.

- *The Federal Commons <www.cfda.gov/federalcommons>.* The Federal Commons is an Internet grants-management portal serving the grantee organization community. Coordinated through the Inter-Agency Electronic Grants Committee,[3] the site is working toward offering all grantees (state and local governments, universities, small businesses, and so on) full-service grants-processing across all functions in the grant life cycle. The site's main feature is a subject-oriented directory to grants information; the subject categories include Agriculture, Health, Business and Commerce, Energy, and Natural Resources, among others. These broad categories are further subdivided into topics under which links to relevant grant information (generally hosted on another organization's Web site) are listed. In the future, the Federal Commons plans to expand its Grant Transactions section to offer the capability to search for grant-funding opportunities across the federal government, and to apply for and report on federal grants.

- *Federal Business Opportunities (FedBizOpps) <www.fedbizopps.gov>.* FedBiz Opps (formerly known as the Electronic Posting System) is a governmentwide Internet-based information system for announcing government acquisitions. It serves industry vendors by allowing them to search for government acquisition opportunities. It also serves government buyers by providing them with the capability to post solicitations on the Internet. The site was designed to be a single entry point for vendors to search government acquisition opportunities across all departments and agencies. The project was begun as a joint effort of the General Services Administration, the U.S. Department of Transportation, and the National Aeronautics and Space Administration, among others.

---

[3]See <http://www.financenet.gov/iaegc.htm> for further information about the Inter-Agency Electronic Grants Committee.

Box 1.2
Examples of State Online Activities

For Citizens

- *Texas.* The Web site of the State Office of the Attorney General allows citizens to file consumer complaints with the office electronically. Individuals simply submit an online form with all the necessary information (e.g., contact information for both parties, a statement of the complaint, and a description of what the citizen thinks would be an acceptable resolution) to begin the complaint-resolution process. The system also allows users to submit copies of scanned supporting documents (in TIF format) via e-mail.[1]
- *Illinois.* The state offers citizens the capability to file their state income taxes online through the state's Web site. The advertised benefits to filing tax forms in this manner include faster processing of refunds (10 days), accuracy (as the system does all the calculations), and availability of the system 24 hours a day.[2]
- *New York.* The Department of Motor Vehicles allows citizens to purchase vanity and custom license plates online, as well as to submit registration renewals. One can search the department's database to check whether or not the desired combination of letters, numbers, or spaces is available, and then purchase the plate online with a credit or debit card. The site even features a rendering of what the user's plate will look like with the chosen characters.[3]

For Businesses

- *Washington.* In March 1999, the state launched a system through which businesses (some of which must pay on a monthly basis) can pay their excise taxes

---

[1]See <http://www.oag.state.tx.us/consumer/complain.htm>.
[2]See <http://www.revenue.state.il.us/electronicservices/ifilefacts00.html>.
[3]See <http://www.nydmv.state.ny.us/cplates.htm>.

This range of experience exists in local government as well; a substantial fraction of municipal and county governments have established some sort of online presence.[6] Still, the committee's examination of crisis management suggests that while some local governments are in a position to lead in the use of IT, there is large variation among them with respect to

---

[6]A survey conducted for the International City/Council Management Association (ICMA) found that among the roughly half of municipal and county governments that responded, more than 80 percent had established Web sites. See Donald F. Norris, Patricia D. Fletcher, and Stephen H. Holden. 2001. "Is Your Local Government Plugged In? High-

online. The Web-based Electronic Filing (ELF) system offers users a fast, simple, customizable, and accurate way to calculate and pay the tax they owe. Using detailed help screens, the system guides users through the appropriate filing processes, eliminating the need for tax filers to wade through large amounts of irrelevant information. The system also offers the capability to postdate filings and payments to better accommodate users' schedules. Payment of taxes is accomplished through the use of an Electronic Funds Transfer (EFT) debit arrangement between the user's bank and the Department of Revenue's bank.[4]

  • *California.* The California Business Portal,[5] an initiative of California's secretary of state, provides information for users who are starting business entities, and it allows them to file related information with the state online. Intended as a "one-stop shop," the site provides access to information on filing requirements and various state forms, and it combines resources from several government agencies and private sector organizations. One of the site's main features is a step-by-step guide to starting a business, offering suggestions on everything from selecting a name for the business to formulating a business plan; a detailed checklist to help users manage each step of the business creation process is provided as well. Among the site's more advanced features is a pilot project that gives businesses the capability to file their corporate "statement of officers" form electronically using a secure server and a credit card. The site also allows users to search through existing corporate records. A link to CalGOLD, <www.calgold.ca.gov>, another California state Web site that presents businesses with information on permits and other requirements of California agencies at all levels of government—including addresses, telephone numbers, and links to agency Internet Web pages—is also provided.[6]

---

[4]See <http://dor.wa.gov/index.asp?/elf/elfcontent.htm>.
[5]See <http://www.ss.ca.gov/business/business.htm>.
[6]For more information, see <http://www.ss.ca.gov/executive/press_releases/2001/01-006.htm>.

technology capabilities. For some, both financial and IT-management resources are very limited.

Altogether, hundreds of e-government initiatives are taking place at the federal level alone. A recent survey found that most federal departments and agencies were engaged in such activities, and more than 1,300 initiatives were reported. Nearly 50 percent were identified as delivering

---

lights of the 2000 Electronic Government Survey" (prepared for ICMA by Public Technology Inc., University of Maryland, Baltimore County), February 27. Available online at <http://www.icma.org/download/cat15/grp120/sgp224/E-Gov2000.pdf>.

information and services to citizens and about 85 percent as making use of the Web.[7]

In this shift toward e-government, commercial third parties are also playing an important role. For instance, the Internal Revenue Service (IRS) accepts electronic tax returns through tax-preparation software vendors. Still, the opportunities and challenges associated with using IT in government are just starting to be addressed. And as IT innovation in the private sector continues apace, the gap between private sector and government practices appears to be growing.

Congressional hearings, reports of the federal Chief Information Officers Council, agency analyses, and similar activities at the state level attest that governments are aggressively exploring how to shape their policies and practices to leverage IT technologies most effectively and to stimulate ongoing innovation and experimentation. For example, the federal government recently established a new central point of responsibility for information technology within the Office of Management and Budget (OMB). Following September 11, 2001, government efforts in information collection, aggregation, and analysis may well expand on a number of fronts, placing corresponding demands for enhancement and flexibility on institutional IT capabilities. At the same time, analyses such as those from the General Accounting Office (GAO) have raised questions about the management and execution of a number of IT programs.[8]

This report examines several questions related to IT research and the use of information technologies in government operations. These questions are raised primarily from the perspective of the relationship between IT research and government IT applications. The aim is to identify approaches that support government in building e-business capabilities analogous to those being developed in the private sector, and in advancing government IT applications such as crisis management and federal statistics. In keeping with its charge from the sponsoring agency, the committee emphasizes in its report the role of IT research, how to structure fruitful interactions between government and the IT research community, and how the research community can help address the leading challenges of e-government. The committee recognizes, however, that a

---

[7]From a summary prepared by the General Services Administration, Office of Intergovernmental Solutions, of its E-Gov Initiatives Inventory. Summary is available online at <http://www.policyworks.gov/intergov/OIS-EGovInventory.htm>, and the inventory database is online at <http://www.policyworks.gov/intergov>.

[8]See, for example, Government Accounting Office (GAO), 2001, *Electronic Government: Challenges Must Be Addressed with Effective Leadership and Management* (GAO-01-959T), GAO, Washington, D.C., July 11.

significant part of the e-government challenge relates to management and implementation challenges associated with deploying *today's* technologies in government.[9] But engagement with researchers offers government an opportunity to better understand where opportunities for innovation lie and to observe and influence the development of the technologies—providing insights that can help government cope with management and implementation challenges.

The scope of this report includes characterization of research needs and opportunities, identification of pertinent research topics, consideration of research-management methods and technology-transition approaches, and aspects of government IT practice that affect the delivery of e-government services. While the focus of the report is the role of the federal government, most of the ideas discussed could apply equally well to state and local governments.[10] The committee also expects that the benefits resulting from the federal government's involvement in and support of IT innovation will likewise apply to all levels of government.

ELEMENTS OF THE VISION

Stimulated in large part by widespread adoption of the Internet and the associated phenomenon of electronic commerce, a broad consensus has emerged in the past several years that governments at all levels can exploit IT to deliver information and services more efficiently and to make

---

[9]The General Accounting Office (GAO) has written numerous reports related to more immediate implementation challenges associated with e-government programs. See, for example, GAO, 2001, *Electronic Government: Challenges Must Be Addressed with Effective Leadership and Management* (GAO-01-959T), GAO, Washington, D.C., July 11. Academic work examining these challenges includes work by the Strategic Computing Program at Harvard's Kennedy School of Government (e.g., Jerry Mechling and Thomas M. Fletcher, 1996, *Information Technology and Government: The Need for New Leadership*, May), the Center for Technology in Government at the State University of New York at Albany (e.g., Sharon S. Dawes et al., 1999, *Four Realities of IT Innovation in Government*, Center for Technology in Government, Albany, N.Y.), and the Center for Research on Information Technology and Organizations (CRITO) at the University of California at Irvine (e.g., Kenneth L. Kraemer and Jason Dedrick, 1996, "Computing and Public Organizations," Working Paper #URB-092, CRITO, Irvine, Calif.).

[10]That research efforts should encompass state and local as well as federal e-government innovation was underscored in Sharon Dawes, Peter Bloniarz, Kristine L. Kelly, and Patricia D. Fletcher, 1999, *Some Assembly Required: Building a Digital Government for the 21st Century*, Center for Technology in Government, State University of New York at Albany, March.

improvements in other functional areas. The nature of these opportunities and challenges has been considered by government bodies, advisory groups, information technology consulting firms, and the like. Box 1.3 lists several of these. Some express the grand view that IT is a principal means for fundamentally reshaping government and democracy, while others focus more on shorter-term opportunities—to enhance the services delivered to citizens and to facilitate enhanced interactions between citizens and government. Somewhere between these two views, there appears to be a general consensus that e-government is a means to such ends as a more informed and engaged citizenry and a more responsive, efficient, and accountable government.

This vision can be captured in terms of a set of generally accepted elements or basic goals. These elements, which underlie the arguments and technical agenda presented in this report and are described below, include the following:

- Satisfying customer service expectations,
- Increasing the efficiency and effectiveness of government operations,
- Providing effective access to information,
- Providing access to a full range of transactions online,
- Increasing participation in government,
- Meeting expectations for trustworthiness, and
- Meeting special challenges in government-unique areas.

Presented in Appendix A are several specific scenarios developed by the committee to illustrate the potential impact of e-government on the daily lives of individuals.

In keeping with the general wisdom that IT should be developed and deployed with all users in mind (internal employees, vendors, and customers), this report considers IT requirements and research needs across each of these user groups.

Satisfying Expectations for Customer Service

Business features such as telephone-calling centers and e-business technologies have given rise to high expectations. Many consumer services are available 24 hours per day, 7 days per week or can be used asynchronously via e-mail and Web communications (that is, with no need for round-the-clock staffing by the service provider). Thus government services, at the very least, are also expected to overcome barriers of time and distance and to be customer-oriented.

One element of responsiveness includes providing citizens with en-

---

Box 1.3
A Sampling of E-Government Objectives

Goals Contained in the Chief Information Officers Council FY 2001 Strategic Plan[1]

Goal 1. All Citizens Connected to the Products, Services, and Information of Their Government

Goal 2. Interoperable and Innovative Government-Wide IT Initiatives

Goal 3. A Secure and Reliable Information Infrastructure that the Customer Can Access and Trust

Goal 4. IT Skills and Resources to Meet Mission Objectives

Goal 5. Collaborations Between the Public and Private Sector to Achieve Better Government

Guiding Principles Developed by the E-Government Excellence Initiative of the Council for Excellence in Government[2]

What should e-government be?

1. Easy to use
2. Available to everyone
3. Private and secure
4. Innovative and results-oriented
5. Collaborative
6. Cost-effective
7. Transformational

E-Government Objective Outlined in the Bush Administration's 2002 Budget Blueprint[3]

Use the Internet to Create a Citizen-Centric Government: The explosive growth of the Internet has transformed the relationship between customers and businesses. It is also transforming the relationship between citizens and government. By enabling individuals to penetrate the federal bureaucracy to access information and transact business, the Internet promises to shift power from a handful of leaders in Washington to individual citizens. The president believes that providing access to information and services is only the first step in e-government. In order to make government truly "citizen-centered," agencies will have to work together to consolidate similar functions around the needs of citizens and businesses. Citizen-centered government will use the Internet to bring about transformational change: agencies will conduct transactions with the public along secure Web-enabled systems that use portals to link common applications and protect privacy, which will give citizens the ability to go online and interact with their government—and with their state and local governments that provide similar information and services—around citizen preferences and not agency boundaries.

---

[1]Chief Information Officers (CIO) Council. 2000. "Strategic Plan: Fiscal Year 2001-2002." CIO Council, Washington, D.C. October. Available online at <http://www.cio.gov>.

[2]Council for Excellence in Government. 2001. "e-government: The Next American Revolution," Washington, D.C., p. 5. Available online at <http://www.excelgov.org/techcon/egovex/index.htm>.

[3]Executive Office of the President (EOP). 2001. *A Blueprint for New Beginnings: A Responsible Budget for America's Priorities.* U.S. Government Printing Office, Washington, D.C., February 28, Section IX, Government Reform. Available online at <http://www.whitehouse.gov/news/usbudget/blueprint/budix.html>.

hanced ways of locating information and performing transactions. Automated phone systems and Web sites able to handle routine information requests and transactions are common in the private sector and are finding increased use in government. But when there are exceptions to the routine, it may be necessary to locate an individual—someone with the required knowledge or authority to make a decision or respond to a particular query. IT can help locate the right individual as well as facilitate communications with that person. Sites may use e-mail to permit the exchange of messages with a customer-service representative, facilitating asynchronous resolution of some problems. These sorts of capabilities are especially important for efficient, effective handling of exceptional circumstances whose resolution requires more than straightforward application of procedures.

It is also now a common practice for commercial Web sites to offer smooth transitions from Web-based interactions with customers to telephone interactions (or chat sessions) with human service representatives. This approach offers advantages to both the site operator and the customer: the customer can rapidly acquire information available on the Web site and, having established context, proceed to click a button on the Web page that provokes a telephone call from a service representative who has knowledge of the state of the customer's interactions with the site. The resulting conversation can thus immediately focus on particular questions without devoting additional time to re-establishing context.

Another element of a responsive service is in-process visibility—analogous to the in-transit visibility that deliverers of express packages offer—which allows one to determine the status of a particular transaction or claim at any given time, thereby making government agency processes more transparent.

Customer orientation also means delivering services in ways that align with the concerns and processes of customers, rather than according to government organizational structure or some other framework that is arbitrary from the customer's perspective. For example, Web sites operated by state and municipal governments offer services for small business operators that present a uniform, business-oriented interface, even though this requires integration of interactions with separate government entities. Business owners, for example, are then freed from having to maintain comprehensive and detailed working knowledge of the roles of the various agencies with whom they must interact—the Web site embodies this knowledge for them. A possible extension of this model would span federal, state, and local governments and even third-party service providers (see Box 1.4).

Box 1.4
An Enhanced "Starting a Business" Portal

What capabilities could a portal dedicated to "Starting a Business" provide to facilitate that process? To help determine the feasibility and best site for a new business, the portal would provide access to such things as econometric, demographic, and trade data; geographic information systems and satellite imagery; information on federal, state, and local regulations for that type of business; and state and local government investment-incentive programs. To help with establishing a business, the portal would permit checking and registration of trademarks and copyrights and online business registration. Once the business was launched, the portal would support payment of withholding for state and federal taxes, social security, unemployment insurance, and the like. Such a portal might also include links to third-party services that could help a business to start up quickly, such as banking, payroll, and tax services.

Increasing the Efficiency and Effectiveness of Government Operations

Although the most visible manifestation of e-government may be in enhancing interactions between government and its customers, the e-government vision also extends to internal operations. Across the political spectrum, it is believed that appropriate use of IT provides a basis for more effective government programs, more efficient work within government agencies, and decreased total program costs. Important IT applications include reducing collection of redundant information, enhancing government workers' access to information required for decision making, and improving workflow management. These interests are reflected in legislation, implementing regulations, and other government initiatives (see the subsection on "E-Government Policy Initiatives" in this chapter).

Providing Effective Access to Information

In carrying out their various missions, government entities collect and retain a great deal of information—information about individuals, businesses, demographic or other statistical data, and material regarding their own activities, rules, and decisions. Government has multiple and occasionally conflicting responsibilities with respect to such information. First, it is charged with keeping a comprehensive historical repository, including long-term preservation of federally generated data and federal decisions. It also has responsibility for providing citizens with access to most government information, though access to certain information is limited by confidentiality rules and other considerations (regarding classified, proprietary, and other sensitive information).

It is useful to classify access to government information in three categories, each of which entails different technical requirements:

- *Effective access to public information.* Online presence or searchability of information is only a first step. "Effective" means that tools and capabilities exist to allow relevant targets to be located in the wealth of government-supplied information. It should be possible to search for appropriate information and resources across government agencies and levels of government without the boundaries being apparent.
- *Access by individuals to information about themselves.* Citizens should be able to review and request revision of personal information with the assurance that only authorized people have access to their records. For example, individuals might examine their own social security and tax records or uniformly update contact information, but this information should be kept private from people other than authorized government personnel.
- *Specialized access to government-gathered or government-held information, under controlled circumstances.* For example, administrative and statistical data are made available to researchers with the aid of technical and nontechnical measures that limit the disclosure of confidential data.

Providing Access to a Full Range of Transactions Online

Citizen and business interaction with government involves an enormous number of different transactions. Many fall into the categories of "very simple" (e.g., purchase a publication) or "routine" (e.g., renewing a car registration or filing a tax return), but interactions with government cover a broad range of complexity. The long-term vision expressed by many (and called for in the Government Paperwork Elimination Act of 1998; see more details in the subsection "E-Government Policy Initiatives" in this chapter) is to make it possible to conduct all government business online. This involves more than simply converting all existing systems into electronic ones, which alone would be a substantial undertaking, given the myriad functions that government supports.

Indeed, a key element of the e-government vision is to provide one-stop portals that integrate across multiple government agencies and levels of government. The goal is to allow users to interact with a wide range of government agencies and officials in seamless fashion, with interactions based on function rather than on organizational details. This can help free users of government services from the daunting task of tracking all government agencies with which they must interact in order to comply, say, with business regulations or tax-reporting requirements. Another aspect of this goal is that users avoid having to re-enter information across multiple transactions or sessions. Such elimination of redundancy is not a trivial issue for the user; consider, for instance, how much of income tax reporting involves copying data from one form to another. Nor is the goal trivial for government to implement. Achieving it will, for example, depend heavily on improving capabilities for protecting privacy, integrating or establishing appropriate authentication capabilities, and providing other safeguards with respect to access to government-held information.

Increasing Participation in Government

Information technology is also a way of providing new means for interactions between citizens and governments—both to improve the interactions and to engage people who have not participated in the past. Providing facilities for enhanced interaction does not *ensure* greater participation, but it is a logical and fundamental step. At the simplest level, such facilities involve e-mail, Web forms, or chat systems to complement the usual mail and telephone channels for communicating with government offices and officials (people might use such means to comment on proposed decisions, inquire about the status of a pending action, and the like). Long-term, the vision extends to enabling new structures that permit greater dialog and more direct involvement with the decision-making process: how can citizens communicate with government officials and with each other to support effective and informed governance? This goal also includes enhancing the electoral process (e.g., by decreasing barriers to voting), while maintaining and improving the accuracy and trustworthiness of elections.

Meeting Expectations for Trustworthiness

It is widely acknowledged that preserving public confidence in the security of government systems is a cornerstone of effective e-government. This was a recurring theme in the workshops convened by the committee and in discussions with individuals within and outside government. The challenge is how to accomplish this goal while expanding and easing access in a rapidly evolving Internet and personal-computing infrastructure. Information requests and transactions often involve the exchange of sensitive information—between individuals and government, between private organizations and government, within government, and among governments at different levels. Protecting the privacy, confidentiality, and integrity of this information against unauthorized disclosure or modification is essential. At the same time, government systems are subject to attack, whether by hackers, terrorists, or nations, which dictates serious attention to information-systems security. With increasing attention to critical infrastructure protection, government interest in trustworthiness will continue to span both government and private sector systems.

Meeting Special Challenges in Government-Unique Areas

For many services, government can build on technologies and processes, already established in the e-business marketplace, that have lowered the barrier for organizations seeking to establish an electronic presence. Most commercial efforts, however, address broadly identified market needs that may not satisfy the requirements of government applications. Such requirements include providing for exceedingly stringent precautions (e.g., for national security or for protecting individual tax records), providing for indefinite persistence of certain archival records (such as those retained by the National Archives), and providing ubiquitous accessibility to certain critical government services (related to social security records, for example). The committee explored two areas—federal statistics and crisis management—in which a number of government-unique requirements are concentrated. Each was considered through an in-depth workshop that brought together domain specialists, particularly those serving in operational roles, with IT experts. (Detailed results of these workshops were published in two separate volumes; [11] the conclusions drawn in this report build on those results.) In both cases, the committee found that specific government-unique requirements presented a mix of longer-term research challenges and shorter-term, more-applied R&D challenges.

TECHNICAL AND PROCESS CHALLENGES TO ADVANCING E-GOVERNMENT PROGRAMS

While in many instances e-government programs can simply build on existing technology and e-business practices, in some areas government leads in demand for IT. Chapter 2, "Special Considerations in E-Govern-

---

[11]For further details, see Computer Science and Telecommunications Board (CSTB), National Research Council (NRC), 1999, *Summary of a Workshop on Information Technology Research for Crisis Management*, National Academy Press, Washington, D.C.; and CSTB, NRC, 2000, *Summary of a Workshop on Information Technology Research for Federal Statistics*, National Academy Press, Washington, D.C.

ment," discusses several specific mission areas for which this is true; Chapter 3, "Technology Levers," discusses a number of more generic research areas where IT capabilities could enhance e-government programs.

As an illustration of the sorts of technical challenges that arise with more aggressive e-government programs, this report considers what is needed to extend interactions with government from information delivery to support for transactions—consolidated services (sometimes known as portals) that enable citizens, businesses, and other government entities to provide information to or engage in financial transactions with multiple government organizations. Some agency Web sites already support a variety of basic transactions with citizens, many analogous to those offered by e-commerce sites. Systems that permit residents to renew driver's licenses and vehicle registration online have been a common area of state focus, reflecting the services' near-ubiquity, the relief from the hassle associated with traditional renewal at state motor-licensing bureaus, and the relative ease of implementing these systems.

Building interagency portals presents numerous technical and management challenges, including these:

- A legacy of information systems supporting numerous government functions, many of which were not designed for interoperability with other systems or for Web-based access (a challenge not unique to government);
- Interoperation challenges arising from working across organizational stovepipes;
- Rules constraining the nature of information sharing across government agencies and programs;
- Funding new online systems while maintaining existing ones;
- Difficulties in identifying and maintaining funding for what are inherently cross-agency activities; and
- Resolving technical issues—such as protocol design, information representation, and security and authentication measures—associated with interfaces that would enable third parties to operate portal sites that interact with government services on behalf of citizens and businesses, permitting third parties to use software that directly connects their own information systems with government services.

Areas of innovation and continuing technical challenge extend well beyond the more visible information and transaction portals. For example, although government has historically provided a great deal of data in electronic form—sometimes directly to the public in easy-to-use formats and sometimes in more esoteric formats that only a few specialized contractors can use—one area of current exploration relates to technology for supporting third-party provision of e-government information and services. The relative roles of the government and private sectors in relation to providing data and information products have long been a subject of controversy. This report does not take a position in this debate, but the committee does note that it would be possible to provide capabilities that more easily permit nongovernment parties (commercial or noncommercial) to provide access to government information and services. Complementing more traditional electronic data interchange technology for interactions between government and larger businesses and organizations, a number of systems for online procurement and grant or contract processing have been rolled out. Finally, there are challenges associated with increasing intragovernment information management and collaboration and with performing such functions across levels of government. In these realms, technical issues such as confidentiality, data integrity, and information management also present significant obstacles.

WHY NOW?

Multiple factors have driven expectations that governments will aggressively exploit IT. The most obvious of these factors is the widespread adoption of technology and related practices in the commercial sector, contrasted with their less pervasive though growing adoption in government. On the demand side, use of the Internet (and other information technology) among the general population has resulted in a rising level of comfort and familiarity with the technologies in other contexts; this fuels expectations that governments will provide services analogous to those in the commercial sector. This growing demand is mirrored in a series of policy initiatives and legislative efforts.

Technology Foundations for E-Government in Place

The recent and rapid growth in e-business is the direct result of two mutually reinforcing factors: (1) a number of technologies reaching points of maturity, scale, and usability at which they can be incorporated directly into the infrastructure of commerce (and government); and (2) the emergence of business practices that can effectively employ these technologies to advantage. A brief review of these technological underpinnings is useful from two perspectives: (1) it illustrates the role that past research efforts have played in providing the foundation for today's e-commerce and e-government, and (2) it illustrates the multitude of technologies that have come together to permit e-commerce and e-government systems to be built.

The most visible technology supporting e-business is the Internet, which has quickly made the transition from research network to critical societal infrastructure. The Internet provides a near-ubiquitous, general-purpose interface across diverse communications links and multiple computing platforms. The World Wide Web, built on top of the Internet, provides hyperlinking among information resources and a uniform user interface for accessing resources located throughout the network. But behind the Web interface, which together with e-mail is the way that most end users experience e-business, lie a number of information technologies that have been developed incrementally over periods of years or even decades. Examples include these:

- *Distributed-processing technologies* that support scaling up to very large numbers of users;
- *Approaches to facilitating data interchange*, including mediator and wrapper techniques (which allow legacy systems to be integrated into newer systems) and the Web-inspired XML standard for describing data;
- *Capabilities for remote service invocation across the network*, which are currently being developed and standardized;
- *Safe mobile code capabilities*, which enable code to be downloaded and run on end-user computing platforms;
- *Database/transaction capabilities*, most notably the development of reliable, large-scale relational databases (and more recent object extensions); capabilities for ensuring integrity and consistency of databases; and the emergence of a standard language, SQL, for querying databases;
- *Multimedia technologies*, including techniques for compressing audio and video, that support streaming or downloaded content and real-time interactions;
- *Graphical Web browsers*, which made Internet services accessible to general users and across a wide range of hardware and software platforms;
- *Search engines*, including indexing, query interfaces, and spiders that build indexes of Web content;
- *Data mining*, which allows patterns to be inferred and relevant data to be identified from very large data sets;
- *Improved understanding of human-computer interface issues*, ranging from page layout and navigation design to e-commerce transaction support and online collaboration;
- *Public-key and other cryptographic security capabilities* that provide confidentiality and integrity of in-transit and stored data, nonrepudiation of transactions, and the like; and
- *Other security capabilities*, including authentication of users, network monitoring, and intrusion detection.

Growing Awareness and Demand

Confirmation of growing public interest comes from a January 2001 Hart-Teeter poll conducted by the Council for Excellence in Government, which found that about three-quarters of Americans believed e-government should be a top priority for the then-incoming Bush administration; and from market research by Deloitte Consulting that projected significant growth in customer demand over the next two years.[12] Actual demand has also been growing, as illustrated by the inclusion of the Internal Revenue Service's Web site, <www.irs.gov>, in Jupiter Media Metrix's February 2001 "Top 50 Web Sites" ranking.[13]

With image and economic development at stake, competition among governments at the state and local levels to deliver improved services is high, a point emphasized by the then-director of the Washington State Department of Information Services, Steven Kolodney, in his remarks to the committee. Internationally, a number of other nations are developing and deploying e-government services. These efforts are at varying levels of maturity, with the more advanced featuring national e-government portals designed to offer a single point of access to both information resources and transactions.[14]

As these pressures result in more services being deployed, conflicting demands will arise for increased reliability; for anywhere, anytime, any-device access; for accuracy and timeliness of information; and for privacy and security of confidential information (these trade-offs are discussed in Chapter 2, "Special Considerations in E-Government").

Finally, interest in e-government is also driven by the desire to increase efficiency in government. Ever-present budgetary pressures, especially on the so-called discretionary portion of the federal budget, have prompted legislators and those in the executive branch alike to seek ways

---

[12]Deloitte Consulting and Deloitte and Touche. 2000. *At the Dawn of e-Government: The Citizen as Customer*, March 1. For more information, see <http://www.deloitte.com/vc/0,1323,sid=2228&ar=&cid=3446,00.html>.

[13]Jupiter Media Metrix. 2001. "Jupiter Media Metrix Announces U.S. Top 50 Web and Digital Media Properties for February 2001" (press release). Available online at <http://www.jmm.com/xp/jmm/press/2001/pr_031301.xml>.

[14]For example, building on earlier efforts to make information and forms available online, France launched its <mon.service-public.fr> portal in late 2001. Development is slated to continue through 2005. See Rory Mulholland. 2001. "French Bureaucracy Takes Online Leap." *BBC News*, November 14. Available online at <http://news.bbc.co.uk/hi/english/sci/tech/newsid_1655000/1655820.stm>.

of leveraging information technology to decrease the costs of providing customer service and administering government programs.[15]

E-Government Policy Initiatives

With growing awareness of e-government, it is becoming a focus of legislation. Building on the Paperwork Reduction Act of 1980, enacted to decrease burdens on the public from information collection and reporting requirements, and on its subsequent amendments, the Government Paperwork Elimination Act (GPEA) of 1998 (P.L. 105-277) requires federal agencies to provide individuals or other entities the options of submitting information to or transacting with the agency electronically and of maintaining records electronically when practicable. The legislation sets a target date of 2003 for implementation throughout the federal government.

GPEA provides that electronic records and their related electronic signatures not be denied validity merely because they are in electronic form, and it encourages the federal government to use a range of electronic signature alternatives. The Clinger-Cohen Act of 1996[16] shifted responsibility for IT acquisition from the General Services Administration to individual agencies. It established the role of chief information officer (CIO) in executive-branch agencies—giving the CIOs both strategic and operational responsibility for all IT programs—and it gave the Office of Management and Budget responsibility for setting overall policies and reviewing agency IT programs through the budget process.

A number of additional legislative measures have helped propel e-government. For example, the FY 1999 Department of Defense Authorization Act requires DOD to establish a defensewide electronic system for ordering supplies and materials, and the Electronic Benefit Transfer Interoperability and Portability Act of 2000 (P.L. 106-171) requires the U.S. Department of Agriculture to establish a national standard for electronic

---

[15]While this effect is widely accepted as an article of faith, economists have struggled to substantiate it. In recent years, some economists have reported that this failure may have been an artifact of the measures selected. For instance, some of them may not have adequately captured any productivity growth manifested in increased output quality rather than quantity. There is a general sense that productivity depends on careful execution of IT programs, often in conjunction with business-process changes. This issue is discussed in CSTB, NRC, 1993, *Information Technology in the Service Society: A Twenty-First Century Lever*, National Academy Press, Washington, D.C.; and CSTB, NRC, 1998, *Fostering Research on the Social and Economic Impacts of Information Technology*, National Academy Press, Washington, D.C.

[16]Formally, the Information Technology Management Reform Act (P.L. 104-106).

food-stamp benefit transactions. A series of hearings on e-government issues were held in the 106th Congress, and new e-government legislation has been under consideration in the current, 107th Congress. Legislative proposals being actively considered as of this writing include establishment of a fund for innovative cross-agency IT programs.

The executive branch has also been the locus of a number of initiatives aimed at advancing e-government. The Clinton administration initiative called the National Partnership for Reinventing Government (originally named the National Performance Review, or NPR), which had the stated goal of increasing the efficiency and effectiveness of government, placed considerable emphasis on leveraging information technology in meeting that goal. The Access America initiative, in part an outgrowth of NPR activities, included several instances of cross-agency collaboration and resulted in the establishment of several targeted portals aimed at particular population segments. Executive branch policy making with respect to e-government has included a presidential memorandum that called on federal agencies to, among other things, make available online by the end of 2000 the forms associated with the top 500 government services. This action resulted in the implementation of the Web site <www. fedforms.gov>.[17]

Another offshoot of the NPR initiative was the Information Technology Innovation Fund (ITIF), which was operated from 1995 to 2000, expiring with the end of the Federal Telephone System-2000 (FTS-2000) program. Funded through a 1 percent set-aside from FTS-2000 charges assessed to agencies, the ITIF provided about $30 million for some 70 programs.[18] A 1996 executive order established the Chief Information Officers Council, an organization of CIOs of the largest 28 federal agencies and two representatives of the smaller agencies, to address IT issues on a governmentwide basis.[19] In addition to setting up an e-government committee in 2000, the CIO Council worked on a variety of issues that

---

[17]Executive Office of the President. 1999. "Memorandum for the Heads of Executive Departments and Agencies (Subject: Electronic Government)." December 17. Available online at <http://www.govexec.com/links/121799memo.htm>.

[18]Projects were selected by a committee of representatives from the interagency body advising the General Services Administration on the Federal Telecommunications System (the Interagency Management Council) and another interagency IT group (the Government Interagency Technology Services Board). Gayle Gordon. 2000. "Information Technology Innovation in the Federal Government" (unpublished).

[19]Executive Office of the President (EOP). 1996. Executive Order 13011. EOP, Washington, D.C.

included Y2K, privacy and security, governmentwide strategic planning, and a number of shorter-term problems.

Attention to e-government has continued in the Bush administration. The president's 2002 budget blueprint includes a small e-government fund for interagency initiatives, with a proposed budget of $10 million in 2002 and total of $100 million over 3 years. The president's proposal would have the fund allocations made by OMB.[20] In October 2001, OMB, with the approval of the President's Management Council, identified 23 priority cross-agency e-government projects.[21] The USA PATRIOT Act of 2001,[22] which is replete with new IT programs and initiatives in such areas as border security, immigration, and airline security, underscores the critical role that IT capabilities are seen as playing in homeland security efforts. In 2002, OMB released a report, which builds on the work of a federal task force convened in 2001, that maps out an e-government strategy and identifies priorities for implementation.[23]

GOVERNMENT IT RESEARCH FOR
ELECTRONIC GOVERNMENT

IT research and development programs exist across the federal government, and many agencies have development programs aimed at creating e-government capabilities. The Digital Government program, an initiative of the National Science Foundation's Computer and Information Science and Engineering (CISE) Directorate, is a program that supports research at the intersection of the IT research community and the operational needs of the government. It aims to help agencies improve internal, interagency, and intergovernmental operations and government-citizen interactions. In particular, the program supports joint research programs between academic researchers and government agencies and requires that

---

[20]See Executive Office of the President. 2001. *A Blueprint for New Beginnings: A Responsible Budget for America's Priorities*. U.S. Government Printing Office, Washington, D.C., February 28. Available online at <http://www.whitehouse.gov/news/usbudget/blueprint/budtoc.html>.

[21]Diane Frank. 2001. "OMB Sets E-Gov Agenda." *Federal Computer Week*, October 29. Available online at <http://www.fcw.com/fcw/articles/2001/1029/news-omb-10-29-01.asp>.

[22]Uniting and Strengthening America by Providing Appropriate Tools Required to Intercept and Obstruct Terrorism Act (USA PATRIOT Act) of 2001, P.L. 107-56.

[23]Office of Management and Budget (OMB). 2002. *E-Government Strategy: Simplified Delivery of Services to Citizens (Implementing the President's Management Agenda for E-Government)*. OMB, Executive Office of the President, Washington, D.C., February 27. Available online at <http://www.cio.gov/Documents/egovreport.pdf>.

at least one government agency be a partner. It encompasses work at the federal, state, local, and international levels. Partner agencies are expected to contribute resources to the collaborative efforts, with the expectation that the program's funding will increasingly leverage additional resources from participating agencies.[24]

Launched in 1998, the Digital Government program has issued grants totaling roughly $30 million to fund more than two dozen research projects and a number of planning grants and exploratory workshops. Funded proposals involve more than 30 federal departments and agencies, some 60 universities and nonprofit organizations, and a handful of commercial firms, and have attracted more than $4 million in matching support from the participating government agencies.[25] Stimulated in part by the availability of federal and state research support, several university-based research centers examining e-government issues have been established.

An offshoot of the Digital Government program is the Digital Government Consortium, a grouping of agencies partnering with IT researchers and/or interested in pursuing future research collaborations. Among other activities it publishes "DG Online," a quarterly that presents news on digital-government developments and related IT research, and maintains the Web site <www.diggov.org>. Another offshoot of the NSF program is an e-government fellows program conducted by the Council for Excellence in Government that is intended to help create awareness of the strategic benefits of and opportunities for collaborating with the academic research community on the part of mid-level government program managers. In addition, the Interagency Working Group on Information Technology R&D has established a program, called the Federal Information Services and Applications Council (FISAC), with the goal of transitioning research results from federal agencies that conduct IT R&D to missions and systems across the federal government. FISAC carries out these activities through several working groups—the IT for Crises Management, Federal Statistics (FedStats), Next-Generation Internet Applications, and Universal Access teams—and through engagement with the NSF's Digital Government program.

---

[24]National Science Foundation (NSF), Directorate for Computer and Information Science and Engineering. 1999. "Digital Government, Program Announcement NSF 99-103." NSF, Arlington, Va. Available online at <http://www.nsf.gov/pubs/1999/nsf99103/nsf99103.pdf>.

[25]Updated from information provided in briefing slides presented to the committee by Larry Brandt, Digital Government Program director, August 3, 2000, and the Digital Government program announcement, cited in footnote 24 above.

2

Special Considerations in E-Government: Why Government Leads in Demand for Certain Information Technologies

Although government can generally build on the technologies and services emerging in the e-business marketplace, special requirements arise in certain areas, reflecting the nature of the government's operating environment. This chapter briefly discusses several areas where government leads in demand for technologies used for e-government services.

UBIQUITY

Governments must provide services to all citizens. Unlike the private sector, they cannot opt to serve only the more profitable customers, nor can they select particular market segments in which to participate (though governments obviously do target specific populations to achieve their policy objectives). Nor can citizens choose which government they wish to deal with.

In the context of e-government, "services" should not be taken to imply only interactions resembling commercial transactions. In government, important services may involve provision of information, for example, or interactions with elected representatives, or commentary from citizens, businesses, and organizations on proposed regulations. Service is provided today primarily through in-person, telephone, and postal mail interactions; but e-mail, the Web, kiosks, and other forms of IT are providing new opportunities to expand the accessibility of services and make them available ubiquitously. Ubiquity has three dimensions: access for everyone, access everywhere, and access anytime.

Access for Everyone

The challenge of providing ubiquitous access to all citizens has several elements. First, it involves overcoming geographical and financial barriers. Much of the excitement associated with e-government is akin to that associated with e-commerce—online access from the home means not having to trek to a government office or find the time to place a telephone call during normal business hours (often only to be put on hold).

But home access is constrained by such factors as the affordability of computer equipment and whether Internet or other telecommunications services are available and affordable in a given area. While the cost of computers has dropped significantly over the years and the penetration of computers and Internet access has reached roughly one-half of U.S. households, the hardware cost is still greater than that of many other consumer appliances; thus penetration lags significantly behind that of telephone service (which is nearly ubiquitous). Similarly, although dial-up Internet access is available from a number of providers in most parts of the country through a local call, there are areas where dial-up access is either not available or only available from a single provider.[1]

Helping provide for those without home access, a growing number of libraries and other community institutions offer public Internet access, supported in part by several federal programs.[2] Residential broadband Internet service provides much higher data rates that support faster download times and the use of richer multimedia content, but its availability is spotty. As this availability continues to grow, there will be concerns about whether those limited to dial-up access will be at a disadvantage similar to that experienced earlier by people without any form of Internet access. Even if affordable and available, today's technologies and services present

---

[1]Thomas A. Downes and Shane Greenstein. 1998. "Do Commercial ISPs Provide Universal Access?" Available online at <http://www.kellogg.nwu.edu/faculty/greenstein/images/htm/Research/tprcbook.pdf>.

[2]The e-rate program, established under section 254 of the Telecommunications Act of 1996, uses a levy on interstate and international telecommunications providers to support discounts on eligible institutions' purchases of telecommunications and Internet services plus internal networking, with discounts varying with location (e.g., high-cost, low-income). Community-based Internet access is also supported by the U.S. Department of Housing and Urban Development's Neighborhood Networks program and the U.S. Department of Education's Community Technology Center grants.

significant usability barriers for those less adept with computers and the Internet. The frustrations of trying to use present generations of systems and software are widely acknowledged to have the effect of discouraging use, especially among less-computer-literate segments of the population. Therefore, at least for the foreseeable future, many people are likely to opt not to adopt these technologies, though they still want access to government services. At a minimum, these gaps suggest that there will of necessity be a long transition period during which new IT-based services will complement but not replace more traditional forms of interaction with government.

With respect to disability or language barriers, computerized services involve both advantages and disadvantages. They present additional barriers to those with vision or motor impairments, given the high degree of dependence on visual communication and the fine motor skills that characterize today's keyboard and mouse-interaction paradigm. But the technologies may also provide the most effective tools to enhance access: online interactions can substitute for visits to a government office, thereby facilitating access to information and services for those with mobility impairments.

Where adequate provisions have been made, it is possible to install modifications or use adaptive software (e.g., text-to-speech or voice recognition) to compensate for disabilities. Recent operating-systems releases and Web software standards contain provisions for this sort of access (such as hooks that allow screen readers or alternative input devices to work with them), and the World Wide Web Consortium's Web Accessibility Initiative has developed both technology and usability guidelines. To maximize the extent to which such techniques are used, legislation was enacted in 1998 that mandates improved access both for federal employees and the public.[3] In addition, rules developed by the Electronic and Information Technology Access Advisory Committee are in the process of being implemented by agencies.[4] When implemented, they will ease, though not eliminate, access issues.

Ubiquity also implies that important information be presented to citizens in a useful and meaningful manner. Simply offering access to government documents is not very effective without some means of conve-

---

[3]Section 508 of the Workforce Investment Act of 1998, P.L. 105-220, which amended Section 504 of the Rehabilitation Act, 29 U.S.C. § 794d. The Americans with Disabilities Act of 1990 extended similar provisions beyond the federal government.

[4]Government bodies working on accessibility include the General Services Administration's Center for IT Accommodation and the U.S. Department of Defense's Computer/Electronic Accommodations Program.

niently searching them and cataloging the results. Similarly, providing direct and unstructured access to the wealth of statistical data collected by the federal government does not necessarily constitute meaningful access. For example, one concern of the federal statistics community is that a low level of numerical/statistical literacy in the general population makes it especially important to provide users with interfaces that provide the necessary context and make it easier to interpret the information. It is certainly not feasible (nor affordable) for government to provide all of its information in a form that is understandable to everyone. But for key information and services, there will be expectations that segments of the population not be disenfranchised. One challenge in building systems that provide universal access is doing so without forcing everyone into a lowest-common-denominator situation.

Access Everywhere, Anytime

"Ubiquity" has another meaning in the information technology arena that is also relevant to e-government: it signifies software and infrastructure capabilities that enable individuals to connect and communicate in more natural ways. The vision, to date unrealized, is that applications from different organizations—including government agencies and offices—would work smoothly together and that users would be provided with effectively seamless access to information and services across various access devices and communications links. Moreover, users would be able to obtain information and services from wherever they are located, and they could use a variety of computing devices—not just desktop computers with wired Internet access. In this arena, both the private sector and government are only in the early stages of exploring potential applications and modes of operation.

Use of IT in government applications requires availability and reliability. Even for common, nondemanding applications such as renewing a driver's license, expectations will be high that computer servers and communications links are functioning most of the time. Particular applications such as emergency services and crisis management demand a very high level of reliability and availability.

TRUSTWORTHINESS

Services supplied by government have to satisfy high expectations of security and confidentiality. In this regard, government must provide guarantees that generally exceed those offered by the private sector. Individuals simply will not tolerate unauthorized or accidental disclosure of personal information contained in tax filings, social security records, and the like.

Conventional business practice is to treat trust requirements with a risk-management approach in which the costs of implementing security measures are weighed against the consequences—a calculation that indicates what (small) level of exposure may be acceptable, as zero risk is impossible to achieve. This approach is not easily implemented in a government setting, where the high level of scrutiny leads to a very low tolerance for failure and where stringent security requirements are the norm. Security in both classified and nonclassified systems has long been an area of emphasis in government information policy, as reflected in the Computer Security Act of 1987[5] and the security provisions of OMB Circular A-130.[6]

One essential ingredient of a trustworthy system is the ability to authenticate the identity of someone wishing to access it, whether that individual is a citizen seeking to retrieve personal records or engage in a transaction online, or a government employee authorized to open records.[7] Identity theft has already proven to be a troublesome issue in the private sector, and it is easy to anticipate heightened concerns if it occurred with e-government services. The simplest computer-based authentication mechanisms, commonly used in Internet transactions today, rely on a shared secret, such as a password. But passwords have a number of weaknesses; for example, because they are chosen by users, they are often easily guessed. One way to strengthen such mechanisms is to make the secrets dynamic, such as by using information contained in recent transactions or communications, but this approach also has vulnerabilities.

Public-key cryptography technology provides more robust authentication, though a major challenge is distributing the public keys in a secure manner. A public-key infrastructure (PKI), which encompasses technologies, processes, and policies, makes use of certificates that allow the identity of users to be authoritatively associated with their public key. One PKI model relies on trusted third parties, known as certificate authorities,

---

[5]The Computer Security Act of 1987 (P.L. 100-235).

[6]Office of Management and Budget (OMB). 2000. *Management of Federal Information Resources*. OMB Circular A-130. November 30. OMB, Executive Office of the President, Washington, D.C. Available online at <http://www.whitehouse.gov/omb/circulars/a130/a130trans4.html>.

[7]The importance of adequate online authentication and lack of a good solution was apparent in the 1997 Social Security Administration's stumbles in providing online access to Personal Earnings and Benefit Estimate Statements (PEBES).

who themselves use public-key cryptography to digitally sign certificates that bind the identity of subscribers to a public key. But full-featured PKI systems are not yet commonplace in either the government or the private sector. Obstacles to widespread use include the complexity of key management; the need to establish systems and procedures for issuance and revocation of certificates; the lack of compatibility among different implementations; and the cost, inconvenience, and system-performance penalties associated with PKI systems' use. Design choices must balance such tensions as ease of use versus security and accountability versus privacy.

Several federal agencies are currently working to develop or implement PKI systems, complemented by cross-agency PKI efforts by the Chief Information Officers Council.[8] For instance, the Department of Defense is rolling out the Common Access Card, which uses PKI technology to issue certificates to military, dependents, civilian employees, and some contractors. Challenges in implementing PKI in government include justifying the cost premiums associated with being an early adopter, enabling the necessary level of interoperability among systems and across agencies, developing systems that scale up sufficiently, and funding and sustaining a cross-agency effort. Government pilots will also provide insight on important operational issues such as how frequently cards are lost or stolen and how well these circumstances can be handled through certificate revocation.

In the development of authentication services, technology, policy, and management considerations are tightly intertwined. In the United States, there has been long-standing opposition to government-issued universal identifiers, as evidenced by the absence of a national identification card (though the issue resurfaced in 2001-2002 in the wake of the September 11, 2001, terrorist attacks).[9] The reality is that each person establishes a number of different identities for interacting with businesses, organizations, and government bodies, and that each of these organizations limits the information that it discloses. For instance, a driver's license is used for a different purpose and is associated with information different from the purpose and information related to a voter-registration card, and there is

---

[8]General Accounting Office (GAO). 2001. *Information Security: Advances and Remaining Challenges to Adoption of Public Key Infrastructure Technology*. GAO-01-277. GAO, Washington, D.C., February.

[9]For an assessment of technology and policy issues associated with national identification systems, see the forthcoming Computer Science and Telecommunications Board (CSTB) interim report on nationwide identity systems. The report will be available from the CSTB home page at <http://www.cstb.org>, as well as the National Academy Press Web page at <http://www.nap.edu>.

little need for exchange of data between the respective authorities. Reflecting concerns about privacy implications, record linkage by government has in fact long been limited by law.

With electronic records, however, it becomes much easier to use identifying information (such as name, address, or social security number) to match records across multiple identities and different government programs. Although there will inevitably be pressures for e-government systems to mirror the complex web of authentication and identity mechanisms found in the paper-based world, trade-offs will be required. These pressures must be balanced against increased complexity that could reduce the utility of e-government systems and compromise their ease of use.

The committee's exploration of crisis management pointed to the need for dealing with exceptions with respect to who can access information and systems. In a crisis situation, access to a variety of private and/or government confidential records may be needed—such as quick access to the blueprints of a building that has collapsed in an earthquake or to medical records needed for emergency treatment—although it would be more tightly restricted under normal circumstances. With electronically protected records, one needs explicit mechanisms for handling exceptions in an emergency. Simply persuading someone holding needed information of the urgency of a situation, which is how such contingencies are typically addressed with paper-based records, might not suffice, as this request alone would not permit records to be unlocked. More generally, tools supporting adaptive policies will be needed in order to accommodate crisis situations, for both enabling additional access (to provide adequate response) and shutting down certain kinds of access (to avert new threats).

Additional trust issues arise if software agents that purport to act on behalf of an individual are used. First, if a user grants authority to an agent to act on his or her behalf, what kind of trust can that person have that the agent will not abuse the authority? This issue requires both validating the code and the environment within which the code will operate with the user's authority. Second, when allowing code to run in one's own environment (e.g., downloading code that will do useful things on one's own local machine), how does the person trust that the code will only do what it purports to do and not, for example, gain unwanted access to personal information stored on the computer? Two approaches have been developed for trusting code distributed over the Internet from servers to clients: (1) have the source authenticate the code before it is run (the approach used with Microsoft's ActiveX controls), or (2) run the code in a special "sandbox" environment that limits what the code is able to do. Of course, there are potential weaknesses in both approaches—such as misappropriated credentials in the case of ActiveX or bugs in the code implementing the sandbox in the case of Java. Thus, it remains an open question whether citizens will trust software agents to provide information and services in such critical areas as tax or health care or feel comfortable running mobile code on their own machines.

Another dimension of the trust issue relates to the consequences of inadvertent information disclosure. Given the authority associated with government data, premature release of, say, a key economic indicator could have significant implications for financial markets. (This was the concern raised in 1998 when the Bureau of Labor Statistics inadvertently posted employment numbers to a bureau Web site in advance of the correct release date and time.)

While such tensions arise in the private sector as well, the long history of public concerns over the potential ability of government to gather and correlate information about individuals means that the government will continue to play a key role in how these tensions are addressed. Research alone cannot resolve them, of course, but it can create technologies that enable greater flexibility. For example, technological tools can enable adaptive policies such as mutually trusted intermediate agents.

ACCESS AND CONFIDENTIALITY

Government collects some information on a strictly confidential basis (e.g., answers to statistical surveys), and other information is collected under the assumption that it will be carefully guarded. Both overall and specific statutory and regulatory restrictions control how such information is used or released publicly, reflecting very strong expectations that the promise of confidentiality will be upheld. Yet at the same time, government is charged with releasing information and making it uniformly available to all.

Disclosure-limiting practices and technologies are required when individuals (or organizations) provide data under confidentiality pledges—promises that if and when the data are released by the government, they will be in a form that does not reveal the sources' identities. In certain cases, disclosure can be limited to carefully selected individuals (e.g., those who have agreed to disclosure terms or who are sworn employees accessing the data for internal government purposes). By contrast, an organization conducting a marketing survey, for example, is not bound to the same requirements.

Governments are also expected to protect the privacy of citizens—to include safeguards on what information is collected and how it is used. A basic privacy framework for the federal government is provided by the Privacy Act of 1974 (P.L. 93-579), which applies principles of fair information practice to federal agencies. As illustrated by the concerns expressed over government Web sites that tracked user behavior by using cookies (small files created by Web browsers to preserve information across Web sessions, providing such capabilities as tracking users' access across Web sites or correlating separate visits to a single Web site) and by the subsequent 2000 OMB memorandum laying down strict conditions for cookies' use—government experiences significant pressures to maximize the privacy accorded to those using government systems and services. An ongoing challenge is providing citizens with assurances that these policies are being fulfilled.

STRUCTURAL CONSTRAINTS

Businesses are competing to meet customer needs better and are tailoring their market segmentation (identification of customer groups such as small businesses or students) accordingly. For electronic services, this usually means coevolving e-business technology and business models. Improvement in customer focus is often accomplished by changing processes and organizational structure to support business needs better—facilitating in particular the creation of portals for information and transactions that are aggregated around the needs of specific market segments. For example, businesses can reorganize to bypass intermediaries in relationships (so-called disintermediation).

Government has been taking some initial steps in this direction as well, as evidenced by multiple government information portals and an increasing number of aggregate transaction portals. Difficult in any setting, modification of processes and organizational structure in government is often significantly constrained by legal and administrative strictures. For example, information-sharing barriers have been legislatively established to protect citizen privacy. A further complication is that the desired span of aggregation can include state and local governments as well as federal agencies. These factors raise the possibility that, rather than reorganizing itself, government might adopt technology to offer integrated user-oriented services. For example, one might create portals that aggregate information or services for the customer and dispatch the elements of the query or transaction to the appropriate set of government entities.

Significant privacy challenges are also posed by portals for government information and transactions that are operated by third parties. Though a competitive market of third-party portals could result in improved access to government services, they will face the issue of how to provide legal and technical safeguards relating to confidentiality and integrity of information that citizens enjoy when interacting directly with the government. For example, the privacy (and compliance) of a citizen is enhanced by laws that prevent certain government entities (such as the Bureau of the Census or the IRS) from sharing information with other government entities. This means that potentially no one but the citizen would be legally able to fuse the multiple data streams provided to the various government entities. The issue is what privacy safeguards can be provided when the citizen presents a broad range of data to a portal operated by a government entity or a third party, in order that the portal operator may appropriately transact on the citizen's behalf with multiple separate agencies.

IT IN SUPPORT OF GOVERNMENT FUNCTIONS

This section provides a brief overview of two areas—crisis management and federal statistics—explored by the committee, and it also takes note of several other government application areas in which government leads in technology demand. This presentation is not intended to be comprehensive. Rather, it is meant to provide an illustration of the sorts of unique requirements that arise in the government sector.

Crisis Management and Homeland Defense

Crises include natural disasters (e.g., hurricanes, earthquakes, floods, and fires) and man-made disasters (e.g., industrial accidents, infrastructure failures, and terrorist attacks). Crises can put lives at risk and pose significant economic threats. The escalating costs (both human and economic) of natural disasters, reflecting in part the increased population living or working in areas at risk, underscore the importance of enhancing "crisis management" capabilities. The September 11, 2001, attacks have led to greater attention to preventing, detecting, and responding to terrorist attacks. Crisis management encompasses crisis response—the immediate activities in the wake of a disaster—as well as the longer-term "consequence management" activities associated with addressing disasters past, present, and future to improve planning, preparedness, mitigation, and recovery efforts.

By its nature, crisis management is a very challenging process. It draws on the capabilities and resources of multiple organizations, including national, state, and local government, nongovernmental organizations, and the private sector (and, depending on the location and scale of the disaster, on international organizations and other national governments). Efforts may encompass many functional areas, including transportation, communications, public works and engineering, firefighting, law enforcement, mass care, health and medical support, urban search and rescue, hazardous materials management, food supply, and energy supply. Information technology needs include telecommunications, information management, geographic information systems, remote sensing, and models and simulations.

As explored in more detail in the committee's earlier report on a workshop examining crisis management,[10] government's particular technological needs include these:

- Robust, high-performance communications infrastructure that can adapt to changing demands, manage traffic congestion, and permit priority overrides for emergency usage;
- Temporary infrastructure that can be quickly deployed when extensive damage has occurred;
- Data management and delivery mechanisms that can function even when the communications infrastructure is degraded and that support unanticipated information needs;
- Composition of information and communications systems in ad hoc situations, such as the establishment of an "instant bureaucracy" for crisis response and recovery (see Box 2.1);
- Improved interoperation of information systems, including that among systems operated by all levels of government and by private organizations (see Box 2.2);
- Support for effective decision making and coordination in the face of uncertainty and stress;
- Overcoming of language and other barriers to communicating with citizens;
- Enhanced means of warning populations at risk, especially providing information targeted to local circumstances faced by individuals or neighborhoods; and
- Adapting of e-commerce technology and practices to accommodate the exception-handling necessary in crisis situations.

Federal Statistics

Federal statistics on population characteristics, the economy, health, education, crime, and other factors play a key role in a wide range of policy, business, and individual decisions. The decennial censuses—along with related estimates that are produced during the intervening years—

---

[10]Computer Science and Telecommunications Board (CSTB), National Research Council (NRC). 1999. *Summary of a Workshop on Information Technology Research for Crisis Management*. National Academy Press, Washington, D.C.

Box 2.1
"Instant Bureaucracy" Capability for Crisis Response and Recovery

One way to assist affected citizens in gaining access to needed information and services in the wake of a crisis might be to provide the means to build, on the fly, a portal that links information and resources from federal, state, and local agencies; nongovernmental organizations; and businesses. In the event of a hurricane strike, for example, such a service might provide individuals with information on evacuation routes and available shelters, allow people to apply for federal disaster assistance, access relief services, file insurance claims, and so forth. At the same time, it would provide capabilities that support decision making and that coordinate actions and resources among federal, state, and local agencies and nongovernmental organizations. Such a service would be accessible via multiple channels, including the Internet, from kiosks (including ones quickly set up in or near a disaster area), and wireless devices. The technology for "instant bureaucracy" would take the form of a toolkit for rapid ad hoc assembly of a portal to support response to a crisis. The following would be components of the toolkit:

- Software tools for such things as authentication of users, access control, data integration, and query across multiple databases;
- Standards for data exchange among systems and agencies; and
- Personalization/persistence capabilities that would retain state between transactions, thereby permitting users to reuse previously captured information and resume interrupted sessions.

---

drive the allocation of federal funding to state and local governments and the apportionment of legislative districts. Federal statistical data are used to adjust wages, retirement benefits, and other spending, and to provide insight into the status, well-being, and activities of the U.S. population.

The surveys conducted to derive this information are extensive undertakings that involve the collection of detailed information, often from large numbers of respondents. Most executive branch departments are, in one way or another, involved in gathering and disseminating statistical information. About a dozen agencies have statistics as their principal line of work—the two largest are the Bureau of the Census in the U.S. Department of Commerce and the Bureau of Labor Statistics in the U.S. Department of Labor—and others collect statistics in conjunction with activities in particular areas.

These federal statistical agencies are characterized not only by their mission of collecting statistical information but also by their independence and commitment to a set of principles and practices aimed at ensuring the quality and credibility of the information they provide. Thus, these agencies aim to live up to the trustworthiness expectations of citi-

Box 2.2
Enhanced Capabilities for Rapid Exchange of Information Across
Levels of Government and with Nongovernment Organizations

Under the rubric of "homeland defense," a number of cases involve interest in building enhanced capabilities for exchanging information among diverse actors, including government agencies at all levels as well as private organizations. Early detection of biological attacks, for example, depends on rapid gathering of information assembled by doctors, hospitals, medical laboratories, and local and state health officials. Detecting misuse of student visa programs to gain entry to the United States for illegitimate purposes requires correlating student visa applications, immigration entry information, and college attendance records. In each of these cases, there is technical complexity in terms of needing to draw on multiple databases systems that are operated by distinct organizations and do not necessarily conform to any common standard. Also, sensitivities are associated with information exchange in each case—both medical and educational records have privacy expectations (and specific legal and procedural safeguards) associated with them. The following technologies would help enable these capabilities:

• Middleware agents that issue standing queries into local databases and send the results to a federal agency. For example, agents could periodically pull specified student enrollment information from university databases and transmit it to the appropriate federal agencies.
• The means for organizations to audit the information transferred to federal agencies, to provide assurance that privacy safeguards are being upheld.
• Tools for anomaly detection based on information drawn from multiple databases.

zens so that people will continue to participate in statistical surveys, and to meet the expectations of decision makers who rely on the integrity of the statistical products they use in policy formulation.

Confidentiality protection and trust take on particular importance in federal statistical data collection: information records are linked and data are combined across agencies (subject to statutory and regulatory constraints), and the resulting statistical products are made available to the public as well as to specialized users. Those providing the information want assurances that it is properly protected. The federal statistical system leads demand for IT in other areas as well. For example, because the data sources and users are extremely diverse and heterogeneous, one cannot rely on a simple system for retrieval and integration. Survey data collection technologies were another example of government leading demand for IT cited at the committee's workshop; federal data collection efforts frequently exceed private sector efforts both in scope and complexity.

Military Applications

Military applications have been a dominant focus of IT research for more than 40 years. The military was, and continues to be, an important customer of IT vendors, and military-funded research programs have provided a considerable fraction of academic research funding. The demanding information-management, analysis, and communications needs of national defense have been reflected in research programs addressing such areas as survivability, security, interoperation, life-cycle management, software engineering, embedding, networking, wearable computing, systems research, modeling and simulation, communications (including support for mobility), and high-performance computing. Progress made in these research programs not only has enhanced defense systems but also has stimulated advances in the commercial computing sector.

Archiving

Government is charged with preserving records of its activities. At the federal level, the National Archives and Records Administration (NARA) has overall responsibility for archiving, and it provides guidance and assistance to agencies on the creation, maintenance, use, and disposition of government records. Each federal agency is responsible for ensuring that its records are created and preserved in accordance with the Federal Records Act of 1950.[11] A combination of pressures to reduce costs, enhance access, increase efficiency, and modernize aging technical infrastructures has contributed to a shift to government information resources being "born digital."[12] NARA and the agencies are challenged by the increasing amounts of material that either originates as or is converted to digital formats. Another agency whose central mission faces pressure as materials are increasingly born digital is the Library of Congress.[13]

As elsewhere in government, expectations on the part of both the

---

[11]Federal Records Act (44 U.S.C. 2904), as described in GAO. 2000. *National Archives: The Challenge of Electronic Records Management*. GAO/T-GGD-00-24. GAO, Washington, D.C. Available online at <http://www.gao.gov/new.items/gg00024t.pdf>.

[12]The answer to whether this shift will realize cost savings, especially in the short term, is not straightforward. Major reports still must be published in paper form, and all of the writing and editorial costs remain the same regardless of format. In addition, there are costs of preparing files for the Web and costs associated with maintenance and connectivity of Web servers. The cost of printing a report may decline as more people use its online version, but it could well turn out that the total cost of providing the report increases.

[13]CSTB, NRC. 2000. *LC21: A Digital Strategy for the Library of Congress*. National Academy Press, Washington, D.C.

general public and specialized stakeholders for archiving are being increased by what is available on the Web in nongovernmental contexts. This shift, together with rapid technological change, challenge existing archival practices and the institutions responsible for providing long-term access to government information.

In the past, standardized publication and filing systems were used to manage at least key documents, facilitating archiving. Today, the situation is more informal, with a considerable body of material residing either on internal systems or on agency Web sites. Efforts to establish governmentwide systems for such digital information have had limited success. Electronic documents are frequently changed over time, and methods for tracking changes or validating the authenticity and integrity of archived electronic documents require further development.

The advent of digital material also raises many new questions about what is worth archiving, especially with respect to files with dynamic content. Web sites come and go (for example, there is no government source for the Clinton administration's version of the White House Web site <www.whitehouse.gov>). With paper documents, one might choose to retain only final documents such as memoranda and not interim documents such as rough drafts and phone logs. With digital information, how does one select—or even distinguish among—materials for archiving? Technologically, it might be easier to keep all e-mail or all distinct draft documents rather than to be selective, but to make sense of this plethora of material (much of which might be superfluous) would place a greater burden on the archivist. Could techniques be developed to automatically select and archive appropriate content?

Even when material is selected for archiving, a key challenge is that while some government systems make provisions for upward compatibility, obsolescence of the associated hardware and software and the fragility of physical storage media pose the risk that digital information will become inaccessible over time. Consensus does not exist at present on standard formats or standard metadata descriptors, although efforts to develop and adopt them are underway.

The basic technical challenge is how governments can maintain digital material that is vital for their own operations, for public access, or for future research. The simplest approach is to create a physical artifact (paper or microfilm printout) of digital materials so that they can be preserved using traditional archival techniques. This does not appear to be an acceptable solution. For example, it takes away the very benefits that electronic documents can provide, such as easier search and retrieval. Furthermore, important types of information, such as databases or links among documents, do not lend themselves to paper representation. On the other hand, preservation of digital materials is not a straightforward matter in light of media fragility and system and format obsolescence.

Approaches to preserving digital material include migration of existing digital material to new software and hardware platforms as necessitated by new technology; development of emulators of obsolete hardware and software systems to permit continued access; and development and adoption of long-term standards and descriptive formats with longer life spans. Once digital material has been archived, another key challenge is to construct search and retrieval systems to facilitate access.

3

Technology Levers

THE ROLE OF RESEARCH IN MEETING IT NEEDS

The federal government has been instrumental in developing the field of computing since the early days. One of the first applications of information-processing technology in government was the use of punched cards and mechanical punch card-based tabulation devices, invented by Herman Hollerith at the Bureau of the Census. These devices, used to tabulate results of the 1890 census, led to the ubiquitous use of punched cards as a medium for input, output, and storage for several decades. After World War II, with the advent of larger computers, demanding government missions including national defense, gathering and analyzing statistical data, and operating the Social Security system prompted substantial federal R&D on both hardware and software. The mission of preparing federal statistical data, for example, triggered a number of innovations, including the 1951 delivery of the first Univac (Remington-Rand) computer to the Bureau of the Census to help tabulate census results; development of the Film Optical Scanning Device for Input to Computers (FOSDIC) that enabled 1960 census questionnaires to be transferred to microfilm and scanned into computers for processing; and Bureau of the Census development of the Topologically Integrated Geographic Encoding and Referencing (TIGER) digital database of geographic features covering the entire United States, which served as a foundational data set for subsequent geographical information systems. Indeed, prior to 1960, the federal government was the dominant customer for computers.[1] This federal dominance—or at least heavyweight status—in the IT sector was also manifested in government's investment in efforts to establish federal data-processing standards, a substantial fraction of which was aimed at information systems security (reflecting a long-standing federal interest in this area).

As the commercial market for computing grew in the 1960s, federal support for IT research continued to reap benefits. Over time, government lost its position as the leading customer for computers, but because information technology remained critical to its various missions and because government led demand in many specific respects, federal support for IT research continued. In the 1980s, the Strategic Computing program, for example, was launched in the U.S. Department of Defense (DOD) in order to accelerate the development and transition of information technologies critical to defense applications. Expanding on Defense Advanced Research Projects Agency (DARPA) research aimed at meeting military requirements, and on U.S. Department of Energy (DOE) energy research, NASA space research, NSF basic science, and the mission research of several other agencies, the High Performance Computing and Communications (HPCC) initiative was created in the early 1990s to help address "grand challenge" applications in areas of government interest such as health, education, libraries, and crisis management, and to accelerate innovation in critical supporting information technologies.

The history of federally funded IT research shows that problems motivated by government needs, such as networking and parallel processing, when suitably framed in a well-designed research program have proved to have wide commercial application (as evidenced by the Internet, distributed transaction processing, and data mining). Broad goals were often pursued in order to infuse new thinking into the technology supply chain of vendors and technology developers for a mission agency. Examples of the success of this approach include process separation for security in operating systems (funded by DARPA in the 1970s and 1980s), computational science (NSF, DOE, and NASA in the 1980s), and custom very-large-scale integrated circuit (VLSI) chip design (DARPA in the 1970s and 1980s).

Ideas were transferred to the commercial sector through direct sponsorship, or through employment or entrepreneurship of laboratory re-

---

[1]Computer Science and Telecommunications Board (CSTB), National Research Council (NRC). 1999. *Funding a Revolution: Government Support for Computing Research*. National Academy Press, Washington, D.C., Chapter 4.

searchers. CSTB's report *Evolving the High Performance Computing and Communications Initiative to Support the Nation's Information Infrastructure* (also known as the Brooks-Sutherland report, after the committee's co-chairs)[2] examined the payoff and key lessons learned from federal investment in computing research. The study concluded that this broad and sustained federal support profoundly affected the development of computer technology and ultimately led to numerous commercially successful applications. In turn, this stimulation of the commercial sector provided the means for government to acquire IT to meet its own needs.

The importance of continued investment in foundational technologies, by players across the board, should not be underestimated. Government in particular has a unique and historic responsibility to help "raise the floor" by working in critical research areas that need stimulus. These are areas in which innovation tends to be nonappropriable—that is, entities cannot retain, or appropriate, the value from an invention, and instead the value diffuses broadly. Thus, advances that are nonappropriable may not directly advance the competitive position of any individual commercial entity, though they may create increments of capability that in the long run may benefit all users of a technology. An additional effect of innovation is that it can create market uncertainties—innovations can disrupt the competitive position of established players, and in unpredictable ways. Thus, it may not be in the self-interest of any commercial party to support innovation. (This point is discussed further in the section "Will Industry Do It" in Chapter 4.)

Today, as government looks to continue to stimulate IT innovation and meet its own needs through IT research, three categories of research are apparent, which might be handled quite differently with respect to research management, government sponsorship, and engagement with industry. The categories are these:

1. *Broad infrastructure.* These "platform" technologies are important for all users of IT, whether commercial or government.

2. *Governmentwide use.* There are important developments that could be applied broadly across many government programs but that might not necessarily apply in commercial settings. Many of these technologies fall

---

[2]CSTB, NRC. 1995. *Evolving the High Performance Computing and Communications Initiative to Support the Nation's Information Infrastructure.* National Academy Press, Washington, D.C. An expanded discussion of the lessons from history is provided in CSTB, NRC, 2000, *Funding a Revolution: Government Support for Computing Research,* National Academy Press, Washington, D.C.

in the category of middleware (see the subsection "Middleware" in this chapter).   DOD has made some attempts to develop agencywide technologies in this category (such as the High Level Architecture [HLA] and the Common Operating Environment [COE]).   An example of an unsolved problem here is that of developing one or more authentication schemes that government agencies can use to authenticate citizens for various categories of transactions.   Where government is successful in developing technologies of this sort and stimulating their uptake, wider commercial use may be an important consequence.   But the investment is justified in terms of the government use because there is no established market.

3. *Mission-specific.*   There are many technologies with narrower applicability that address more focused government technical problems.   In the course of the committee's workshops examining crisis management and federal statistics, a number of opportunities were identified where the mission interests of federal agencies and the technical interests of researchers overlap.   Government applications provide not only new technical research challenges but also, frequently, texture, richness, and veracity not easily created in laboratory studies. Working on this class of problems can thus represent a mutually beneficial situation for the researcher seeking to explore an idea and the government body seeking to discover new approaches to solving a particular problem. Research funded by the NSF's Digital Government program illustrates some of these points of intersection, many of them already identified by other federal agencies and computer science researchers (see Box 3.1).   A number of specific applied-research opportunities identified in the committee's workshops are described in its earlier workshop reports.

All agencies with organic research programs undertake research in category 3, above. Those for which IT plays a strategic role also undertake programs in category 2.   Those with a broad stake in the growth of IT (such as DOD, NASA, DOE, and others) also address challenges in category 1, along with the NSF. The NSF Digital Government program is positioned to undertake research in all three categories, forming alliances with mission users in order to identify requirements more concretely, provide access to data and subject-matter experts, and provide potential for early validation of innovative concepts.

SOME E-GOVERNMENT RESEARCH AREAS

The research areas discussed in the following subsections are drawn from the committee's detailed studies of crisis management and federal statistics, as well as from its less-intensive explorations of other government application domains, reviews of the literature on government IT, and interactions with experts both from within and outside government. The research topics presented in this chapter are intended to provide examples of the kinds of topics likely to be important to government information technology. *It must be noted, however, that inclusion of a topic in this chapter does not mean that it is an area of sole or even primary importance to government.* Many of these issues are important across-the-board—in government and the private sector alike—though the government context may present especially stringent requirements or particularly novel issues or in some other way lead in demand. *In addition, it must be noted that this compilation of topics is not a comprehensive research agenda.* Because the IT requirements across government mission agencies are numerous and diverse, the absence of an area of research from this chapter should not be taken as an indication that it is not worthy of support in the context of e-government. Moreover, lists of pertinent topics will evolve over time as the state of the art advances, requirements in government are modified or become better understood, and other changes occur. Nor could a study of this scope and level of effort present a comprehensive analysis of requirements and gaps governmentwide.

These caveats notwithstanding, the committee intends the compilation of topics presented below to be useful to those seeking to stimulate innovative projects, solicit proposals from researchers, or engage operational government agencies in IT research.

Information Management

Government applications present significant challenges for information-management technology. Governments hold large amounts of heterogeneous data from a wide variety of sources—textual information, demographic data, geographic data, image and video data, and so forth—and in databases with many different schemas. They also present a heterogeneous computing environment, with numerous types of computer platforms, database systems, information retrieval systems, and document-management systems, just to cite a few.

This diversity of computing systems reflects the substantial scale and longevity of legacy investment that is typical of government (and often found in the private sector as well), and the large number of departments, agencies, and programs that traditionally have specified and procured systems without reference to an overall information or systems architecture. Many older systems adhere to obsolete federal information-processing standards. More recent systems adhere to prevailing commercial standards. But agreement on standards is difficult to achieve, compliance with such specifications is never total, standards do not cover the full range of design decisions (especially with respect to semantic issues),

Box 3.1
Research Grants Funded by the NSF's Digital Government Program,
1999-2001

- A Framework for the Dissemination, Use, and Storage of Geospatial Images for Field Data Collection
- A Multinational Investigation of New Models of Collaboration for Government Services to Citizens and Businesses
- A Planning Proposal: Quality Graphics for Federal Statistical Summaries
- An Ontology for Geospatial Knowledge
- Challenges in Statistical Digital Government: A Workshop Promoting Agency-Research Institution Interaction
- Citizen Access to Government Statistical Data
- Criteria-Based Inference from Geospatial Data: Automating Government Decision Making for Genetic Food Security, Crop Improvement, and Global Germplasm Needs
- Defining a Motion-Imagery Research and Development Program
- Developing an Information Technology and Organizational Design Research Agenda for the Evaluation and Management of Research Proposals
- Digital Gazetteer Information Exchange (DGIE)
- Bringing Government and Citizens Together: A Metadata Extension Testbed for the Kentucky Spatial Data Infrastructure (KYSDI) Clearinghouse
- Exploratory Research on Transnational Digital Government
- Digitalization of Coastal Management and Decision-Making Supported by Multi-Dimensional Geospatial Information and Analysis
- Geospatial Data-Mining Techniques for a Multimedia Integrated Modeling System
- Heterogeneous Reasoning Tools for Design Support

and, perhaps most significantly, standards evolve over time. In short, standards alone are not a solution to the challenges of information sharing and integration.

Government systems also provide direct support for diverse users and applications—including, for example, commonly required transactions at local, state, and federal levels; requests for information about people and property; requests for historical information (including information retained in official archives); requests for statistical information; researcher requests for various types of information; and government-worker requests. While some systems are intended as servers or only for expert users, others are expected to provide meaningful access to a broader user base. And regardless of their role, information-management systems design must also take into account a basic tension in the government environment: providing access to as much information as possible while protecting system security and individual privacy. This goal can be

- Identifying Where Technology Logging and Monitoring for Increased Security End and Where Violations of Personal Privacy and Student Records Begin
- Information Technology Accommodation Research: Creating a Doorway for Universal Access
- Internet Voting Study
- Knowledge Management Over Time-Varying Geospatial Datasets
- NSF-CNPq Collaborative Research—Issues in the Development of Spatial Spreadsheets and Browsers
- Planning Grant for Research into the Use of Internet-Based Intelligent Systems for Shaping and Enhancing Citizen Participation and Service Delivery
- Regulatory Compliance Reporting at EPA: Moving to Digital Information Acquisition, Exchange, and Dissemination
- Citizen Agenda-Setting in the Regulatory Process: Electronic Collection and Synthesis of Public Commentary
- Evaluating Information Integration Architectures for a National Statistical Data Infrastructure
- Exploratory Research for Correlating and Data-Mining Flight Data from NTSB Accident Investigations
- Social Processes and Content in Intelink Online Chat Data
- Testbed for High-Speed "End-to-End" Communications in Support of Comprehensive Emergency Management
- Workshop on an Urban Research Agenda
- Workshop on Biodiversity Informatics

SOURCE: National Science Foundation Award Abstract Database, October 2001. Available online at <https://www.fastlane.nsf.gov/a6/A6Start.htm>.

challenging to accomplish because there are interactions among system designs even when the systems themselves do not interact—the results of queries to separate systems can be combined externally. These considerations are reflected in a number of research needs, both basic and applied, for systems that access government information:

- Capabilities for finding relevant information in text and extracting structure from text;
- Managing unstructured and semistructured data;
- Finding relevant information in other types of data, including time-dependent data, geographical databases, satellite data, images, video, and audio;
- Providing effective access to heterogeneous information types (e.g., mixed text, image, audio, and geographical data);
- Providing effective access to multilingual information, including

ways of entering queries and searching in multiple languages, including cross-lingual searches; and

  • Representing and managing approximation, uncertainty, and inconsistency.

A second class of problems is that of metadata and interoperability among data sets and information systems. Without agreement on the format and meaning of data (or a means of reconciling different formats or semantics), it is not possible to transfer information from one system to another or combine information from multiple systems. One set of issues concerns information about the data or metadata. For example, metadata about a raw number provides information—such as its scale, accuracy, or unit—that permits it to be interpreted. Interoperation is easier when system designers reach consensus about the metadata. This is primarily a social process, but it involves the technical dimensions of representation and semantics as well.

Representation issues include the syntactic/lexical representation of each individual data item (e.g., a date or name), the record structure for aggregates of multiple data items (e.g., a set that includes a name, social security number, date of birth, and employment start date), and the linear byte-stream representation of that data for transmission over networks and storage on secondary media. Semantic issues include reliability, source, and other attributes related to the quality of the information; the interpretation of the information; and the consistency relationships of that information with other data.

The XML "meta standard" for metadata has been widely embraced because it provides an effective approach to achieving commonalities with respect to the three representation issues just noted. XML itself only provides a language for describing data and relies, therefore, on the success of social processes to obtain consensus on representation within specific domains of common interest. With respect to semantic issues, there is less progress, though the XML standard at least enables communities to "speak" a standardized language in addressing semantic issues. Standardization of the metadata describing the format of databases can be achieved through agreement on XML DTDs (document type definitions, which are formal descriptions of what can appear in a document and how documents are structured), and while not research per se, this is an area deserving continued work. A variety of government and industry bodies are working to develop standards for various application areas.[3]

---

[3]See <http://www.xml.gov/scripts/efforts.cfm>.

Research on semantic issues is taking place in the areas of knowledge representation and agent-oriented computing. While various approaches have been advanced, including mediators and wrappers that act as translators between the format and syntax of one system and another, semantic interoperability is generally viewed as an unsolved problem—or rather, one that can be solved only in increments. The social process of agreeing on metadata that describe the content or the important topics covered by information objects and databases is difficult to standardize but is one crucial element for integrating information resources. This type of metadata is often expressed using a predefined vocabulary, represented as a list of categories or more structured forms such as taxonomies and ontologies. Common ontologies facilitate semantically meaningful integration of data from diverse information sources.

Efforts to agree on standard data descriptions, which are more a matter of implementation than of research, should not be confused with work aimed at developing and merging ontologies for describing content, as well as at tools for ontology building and sharing. Many taxonomies already exist in government agencies, and many others are being created—for example, in the sectors of human resource, finance, and health care. Developing technology to support the development and merging of taxonomies, as well as the application of these taxonomies to information objects, is an important research challenge. As part of these efforts, ways must be found of coping with the evolution of metadata. Another challenge is to find ways to address heterogeneous metadata standards, much as systems must support multiple image or document format standards.

A number of other research issues come up in the area of integrating/fusing information from diverse sources. For example, improved techniques for combining results from different systems (e.g., multiple-text search engines, database systems, geographic information systems) and techniques for presenting those results would all be of value in a government setting.

The design of information systems themselves is an area of ongoing exploration. One recent trend has been the development of centralized data warehouses, which contain data extracted from operational transaction systems, to facilitate retrieval or analysis. Such warehouses could provide short-term benefits, such as improved understanding of the cost of programs and how agencies use resources, and long-term benefits, such as better understanding of the impact of programs and support for enhanced planning of new programs. Frequently, information is stored in multiple systems, which necessitates special techniques for locating and retrieving it. This entails developing improved algorithms for finding information resources, selecting the appropriate sources for a given query, representing their content, and merging the results.

Data-mining techniques offer capabilities for discovering important but nonobvious patterns and relationships among and between a wide variety of data types. These include improved algorithms for data mining of conventional structured databases (including data warehouses) as well as techniques for the data mining of less-structured text data and more complex multimedia data sources.[4] The wealth of data in government information systems presents an attractive opportunity for developing new data-mining techniques, though it will be important to differentiate among user groups. Statisticians or social scientists seeking to explore patterns in demographic data will have a different set of needs from those of nonexperts. Interesting questions include how nonexperts might use data-mining capabilities and how one could make these techniques available to them in a usable form.

Human-Computer Interface

CSTB's 1997 project examining every-citizen interfaces to the nation's information infrastructure underscored the opportunity and challenge of developing technology that could be used easily and effectively by all.[5] Many e-government systems must provide information and services to a range of users: experts within the government, experts outside government, and the general public. Even when the user population is segmented by capability and interest, success in delivering services depends on the development of appropriate human-computer interfaces (HCIs). HCI issues are especially important because there is no Moore's law on human perceptual, attentional, or cognitive/problem solving capabilities—in other words, people's abilities do not scale up at the same rapid rate that basic computing capabilities do (or, for that matter, the rate at which the total volume of information resources is growing). Thus, as Herbert Simon has observed, the scarce resource in human-computer interfaces is and will remain human attention. This is especially true in nonroutine applications such as crisis management.

HCI is an inherently multidisciplinary research area, drawing on ideas from psychology as well as computer science (and related areas such as

---

[4]For example, in its statistics workshop, the committee hosted a discussion of data-mining opportunities using data from the National Health and Nutrition Examination Survey, which collects clinical information in text form as well as in X-ray images.

[5]CSTB, NRC. 1997. *More Than Screen Deep: Toward Every-Citizen Interfaces to the Nation's Information Infrastructure.* National Academy Press, Washington, D.C.

information management). A hallmark of the field is the use of iterative user-centered design (UCD) methods to develop useful—and especially usable—systems. Current UCD methods include early focus on users and their tasks, ongoing empirical measurement and evaluation of the system, iterative design and testing, and integrated focus on the end-to-end systems that considers the larger social context in which they are deployed. HCI professionals are involved early in the design of systems and participate throughout the later stages of system development. Existing UCD methods have been found to work well when there is a limited range of users and tasks, which means that accommodating the greater diversity of individuals and applications in government will likely require extension or refinement of the approach.

Government systems need to be usable by a wide range of individuals and organizations with heterogeneous needs, cognitive abilities, and hardware and software. How can we create systems that allow users, whether they be students, journalists, local community groups, government workers, or policy makers, to access the wealth of government information in a way that is useful to each of them? Providing "universal access" means building systems to work well with a diverse user population and making appropriate facilities available for populations with special requirements—such as disabled citizens, speakers of languages other than English, and those located at remote sites. Analysis of individual differences, and requirements and methods for accommodating them, will play a role. Where some users have low skills and/or little experience, for example, systems that have a high tolerance for human error are likely to be especially valuable.

One particular HCI problem is that of finding, understanding, using, and integrating information of the diverse types found in the multitude of government information sources. Formulating good queries is difficult, and tools that support this process could be improved. Developing advanced systems requires a better understanding of user requirements, information-presentation techniques, information-access strategies, and the development of flexible and modular architectures. A challenge that often comes up in government for supporting decision making, and in government's communications to the public, is how to represent the uncertainty associated with many sorts of data. Because uncertainty reflects sampling and systematic errors (such as results from a statistical survey), known limitations in the model being used (such as a model of earthquake damage), and other extenuating circumstances, it often plays an important role in correctly interpreting and acting on a piece of information.

Computer systems, including those for information summarization and presentation techniques, should exploit knowledge of basic human perceptual and cognitive skills. Because today's interfaces rely on a limited set of input and output capabilities, researchers should continue to push the hardware and software envelopes to support new interaction styles (e.g., richer visualization, perceptual user interfaces, multimodal input, and support for a range of motor and language capabilities). One promising approach for environments in which users interact extensively with data is to provide tight coupling of user actions to displayed results and easily reversible actions. Tight coupling implies low latency, which means that careful attention must be paid to how data transfer and processing are divided between the server and the client. Advances are required at the cognitive level as well, where people's rich but fallible memories and vast amounts of general and domain-specific knowledge often do not match well with the information required by computer systems. A richer range of interaction styles is also important to match the user's environment. At the forefront of all design improvements should be the goal of better leveraging and augmenting natural human capabilities. One example is mixed-initiative systems that support both user-initiated (direct manipulation) and agent styles of interaction.

While there are many HCI challenges related to interactions between a single user and an information system, many of today's systems involve more than one user interacting with local data and applications. Many different communication scenarios of interest exist, including one-to-one (such as when a citizen and a government worker interact), one-to-many (such as when a population at risk in a crisis is being alerted), and many-to-many (such as when a community explores a policy issue). Progress on each of these fronts will require new theories, computing architectures, and design methods to support collaboration, as well as better understanding of the group and organizational contexts of information use. A variety of techniques, such as collaborative filtering, could play an important role.

Particular government applications will pose their own specific HCI challenges. For example, in crisis management, it is especially important that systems be able to support users in carrying out nonroutine tasks and facilitate working in unplanned, ad hoc situations. In the case of statistical data, variability in the public's statistical literacy poses a particular challenge to effective presentation of federal statistical data. While an expert is equipped to locate the information necessary for understanding the limitations associated with a given piece of data (such as sampling error or the implications of particular definitions used in deriving the data), a lay user may not be so equipped; he or she will benefit from HCI approaches that make these factors as intuitively understandable as possible.

Support for decision makers, including systems that help to frame, interrogate, and anticipate the world in such a way as to effectively assist in the decision-making process, is another area for continued HCI work. A user-centric view, for example, allows a decision maker to individually establish the context, pose the questions, control the content, and mold the style of presentation. Related applications include interactive team-decision environments, systems that capture and represent domain expertise, and systems that permit intelligent real-time control.

Network Infrastructure

A variety of infrastructure components provide an important foundation for e-government, starting with basic network-communications capabilities. Internet technologies are in widespread use, and both government and the private sector continue to press the Internet industry to provide yet more—greater capacity, for example, and improved security and reliability. These demands continue to stimulate research and development, which has already resulted in dramatic increases in network bandwidths. But because the R&D challenges are largely common to both the private and public sectors, they are not explored in depth here except to note that in government, as elsewhere, the attributes of privacy, scalability, reliability, and accountability, among others, are highly valued.

If the communications infrastructure is to be available widely, especially for use in interacting with individual citizens, then low-cost, ubiquitous access—enabled in part by continued innovation—will be required. A range of new capabilities might be enabled through the use of the Internet, particularly high-capacity, always-connected broadband access (as opposed to the more typical low-speed, dial-up connections, which incur a delay each time an Internet connection is established). In the short term, deployment will proceed using existing technologies with incremental developments to them. Looking to the longer term, further research on wireless technologies offers the potential for improved performance; and in the area of fiber optics, research could provide designs and architectures with lower deployment costs. The complex economic, implementation, and public policy issues associated with provision of broadband Internet access to residences have constrained deployment more than the state of the technology has.[6]

In contrast to the more routine government functions, domains such

---

[6]See CSTB, NRC. 2002. *Broadband: Bringing Home the Bits*. National Academy Press, Washington, D.C.

as crisis management obviously change the normal demands for communications. Meeting the information requirements of a crisis depends on an infrastructure that can handle above-normal loads at just the time when large portions of it may have suffered physical damage. Whereas for some applications infrastructure can be brought in from outside a disaster area, crisis response would often benefit from having a more survivable infrastructure in situ, and with sufficient headroom for reliable and survivable crisis response.

Crises require the communications infrastructure to adapt to changing demands by managing unusual traffic-congestion patterns, for example, and permitting priority overrides for emergency usage. Such scaling and robustness questions arise in a number of large networks that are key to public safety, such as air-traffic control; police, fire, and safety communications networks; and 911 and other emergency dispatch systems. Priority-access capabilities are already a feature of the wire-line public telephone network. But with increasing use of alternatives to the public telephone network comes increased interest in providing priority, scaling, and robustness capabilities in public wireless networks, the public Internet, and private networks based on Internet technologies.

Several networking-research questions arise from these requirements. Networks that are self-adaptive are, for example, able to rapidly reconfigure themselves—say, as wireless infrastructure elements—in response to a crisis. In particular, networks that could reconfigure themselves quickly under conditions of damage and changes in demand would be of great utility. Even in the absence of extensive self-adaptation, it is better to have an infrastructure that is able to degrade gracefully as its components are affected by a crisis than a system that completely fails.

A research question that addresses the need to prioritize traffic is how to build networks that allow applications to interact with the infrastructure so as to allow the incorporation of capabilities such as priority override features or the recognition and management of information surges during a crisis. Also, it would be useful to develop interfaces that allow the combined deployment of private and public infrastructure, thereby permitting crisis responders to exploit whatever infrastructure elements are available. In any case, efforts should not be confined solely to improving the infrastructure. Modifying the applications themselves can permit them to cope gracefully with less-than-optimal network performance. Designers of applications intended for use in crisis situations cannot assume that there will be large amounts of bandwidth or that connectivity will be available on a consistent basis. Strategies for coping would include adapting the frequency of updates to the available bandwidth or falling back to activities that consume less bandwidth (e.g., transmitting text instead of multimedia data).

Finally, there are opportunities to leverage "push" technologies in emergencies. Providing up-to-date information to large segments of the public is important because it permits people to take appropriate actions, helps prevent panic, speeds remediation efforts, and can prevent follow-on crises. But widespread broadcasts (whether by television, radio, or the Internet) are not necessarily the best approach—they provide only limited, situation-specific information and cannot supply details tailored to the needs of individuals, such as what evacuation route to use. By contrast, push technologies could deliver more focused (and presumably more accurate) warnings and more detailed advice on what actions to take and could decrease the frequency with which people receive false alarms (warnings that do not apply to them).

One approach identified as worthy of further investigation involves "reverse 911" systems, whereby the usual direction of interaction between citizens and emergency managers is reversed. "Call by location" can automatically contact all households and businesses that might be affected by a fire or flash flood, warn them of the impending danger, and instruct them on what evasive action to take. Telephone-based reverse-911 systems are already being used in a number of areas. Increasingly widespread deployment, as well as the use of always-on broadband Internet, wireless data, and similar new communications technologies, present additional opportunities for providing this kind of service.

Information Systems Security

Government applications of IT often center on the management of records about individuals and businesses. Significant savings can be obtained by removing intermediaries and allowing direct access to these records—by the properly identified parties authorized to view them. Similarly, the accessed records are subject to change only by those authorized to make changes. To ensure the security of such systems and promote trust in them by citizens, several services need to be applied: confidentiality, integrity, authentication, authorization, and audit.

Confidentiality

Confidentiality services prevent the unauthorized disclosure of data while the data transit a network or communication link, or while they reside on disk. These services are intended to prevent an attacker, or any other unauthorized individual, from bypassing data-authorization functions. Confidentiality of data is usually provided by the use of encryption—that is, the scrambling of data so that they can only be unscrambled with the use of the correct secret information, called an encryption key.

Secure Sockets Layer (SSL) is one widely deployed confidentiality mechanism. It is integrated with Web browsers and encrypts data exchanged between the user and SSL-protected Web sites.

Integrity

Integrity services protect data from unauthorized modification. Like confidentiality services, they often depend on encryption algorithms, augmented by calculation of checksums in order to detect changes. A digital signature is a form of integrity protection, as its validation shows that the data to which the signature was applied have not been inappropriately changed. SSL also provides data integrity for the messages sent between a Web browser and a server, preventing an attacker on the network from modifying the messages, and thus the data contained in them, without such changes being detected.

Authentication

Several ways exist for validating a user's identity. The simplest is for the server to keep a list of passwords and require that the user enter his or her password. This approach is not particularly strong, and it is difficult to manage, as the user would have to register in advance with each individual system with which he or she might eventually communicate.

Authentication can also be accomplished through the use of an authentication protocol—sometimes based on the use of a private encryption key, known only to the named individual, together with a certificate issued by a trusted third party that associates the encryption key with the user's identity (digital signatures are one example of this form of authentication). In other cases, authentication is based on other forms of encryption with keys that are also distributed by a trusted third party (Kerberos authentication is an example).

The use of third parties for authentication, whether these are certificate authorities in the public-key infrastructure or authentication servers in Kerberos, requires that these services be trusted, both by the government systems accepting authentication and by the users whose identities are being authenticated. This is where many of the problems associated with the establishment of public-key infrastructure have been experienced. There is no single authority trusted by everyone, and as a result, many organizations (for example, banks) require separate registration by users so that only the bank's own servers are relied upon.

The establishment of a single government authority to authenticate users presents privacy issues, because this authenticated identity becomes a unique identifier. Letting the government rely on authentication authorities in the private sector also presents possible security problems, however, as a user might obtain a certificate fraudulently (this is not to say that users could not do so with a government certificate authority). Ultimately, it will likely be the case that multiple authorities are supported and that authorization policies will dictate which ones must be used in particular contexts. When signing up for a service, the user would specify or accept the default for which authorities may be relied upon for subsequent authentication. This leaves unanswered the problem of how the user would authenticate his or her first contact with a particular agency.

Authorization

The end point of security services is authorization: controlling access to only those entitled. Other security services play supporting roles, either in helping to make the authorization decision (as is the case with authentication) or in preventing individuals from bypassing the authorization mechanisms to access or modify data through other means (prevented by confidentiality and integrity services). Even audit, described below, relates to authorization, as the goals of the audit mechanism are to assure in retrospect that appropriate policies were enforced by the authorization mechanisms and to find weaknesses.

While the basic technologies are reasonably well understood, their deployment and operation at large scale are not. One example of the sort of poorly understood issue that arises at large scale is policy management, which is one of the hardest aspects of creating secure systems. In fact, many security breaches result from either the misapplication of security policies, or the use of security policies that are not appropriate in particular contexts. Writing correct policy requires a thorough understanding of how a system is to be used and how it is not supposed to be used. While creating consistent policies in a single system is hard enough, creating them in government systems is likely to be even harder—especially when the policies are concerned with the exchange of information between agencies. This is the case because there are likely to be numerous legislated policies and procedures specifically associated with each agency, many of which might not be consistent with one another.

The whole issue of exception access is another aspect of security policy that must be considered. For example, one might want to create policies that allow access to data in certain crisis situations, such as a building fire or medical emergency, that is otherwise not allowed. If the data are stored in a computer system, then these exception policies must be part of the policy base enforced by the system, further complicating the problem of policy management. Such policies must allow exception access, but in a limited way, so that the security of the entire system is not compromised.

One of the most effective ways to defeat security is the practice of "social engineering." For example, a perpetrator calls and explains that there is a truly unique emergency, requiring urgent access to the records. This is how many hackers, spies, and thieves gain unauthorized access. So if a system is constructed to simply weaken access policies in an emergency, then as a consequence it can also become easier to intrude through social engineering—there is a trade-off between efficiency of operation and efficacy in crisis situations and security and safeguards. Improve one, and the other gets worse. In the end, the weak link is always the human element—not because humans are faulty, but rather because the procedures put in place as safeguards often end up thwarting those who must use them on a continual basis.

To date, most support for policy management is done on a custom basis for each application, creating stovepipe security systems that are inflexible, difficult to understand, and present many weak links for an attacker to exploit. Work is underway, for example, on the Generic Security Services Application Programming Interface, to create common interfaces for authorization, but the results of such efforts will not be useful until one starts to see integration of these interfaces with a wide range of commercial systems.

Audit

Audit mechanisms are important for improving the public's confidence in security systems because these mechanisms provide a way to record the kinds of access that were granted; they allow administrators to take action after the fact when access rights have been abused, and thereby to correct the problem. Audit mechanisms will be of particular importance for any exception policies that are used by emergency workers or by others with authority to override normal access protections. For someone with exception access, knowledge that his or her use could be scrutinized helps deter abuse of such access. To be most effective, the audit mechanism for exception access should generate reports that are submitted to the person whose data were accessed.

Audit also applies to the configuration management of systems, which is the effective monitoring of the integrity of software components, hardware devices, and supporting configuration data. Some viruses and worms, for example, exploit vulnerabilities that were created by previous infections of other viruses and worms. In addition, configuration management can detect failures in upgrading in response to security updates. Indeed, many users and systems administrators lack the tools to detect whether systems software has been compromised or even whether new (and unwanted) software applications have been installed on agency or corporate systems.

E-Commerce and Related Infrastructure Services

E-business depends heavily on a number of services that run on top of the basic communications fabric discussed above, including these:

- Information dissemination services, such as Web servers and push technology;
- Communication services, such as e-mail and instant messaging;
- Directory services, which provide for referencing and retrieval of collections of personal information (e.g., name, organizational affiliation, and e-mail address or mailing address) as well as information such as who is authorized to perform which functions in an information system; and
- Security and identification services, which permit information systems to be secured, users of those systems to be authenticated, and access to be authorized.

Some of these services, such as Web servers, e-mail, and basic directories, are all relatively mature technologies; the government is likely to be able to leverage commercial-sector developments in them. One related area in which government generally needs to pay more attention to research, however, is that of how to build a very-large-scale authentication infrastructure (e.g., a public-key infrastructure that supports all citizens). Another is back-end information-management challenges related to tying together multiple systems feeding a Web site (such as building ontologies to bridge the stovepipes in different agencies). Specific research issues with respect to these areas are addressed in other sections of this chapter.

In addition to enhancing its own transaction-support capabilities, the government has an opportunity to promote the development and use of common transaction mechanisms to widen access to government-supported services. Citizens would then be able to select a third-party intermediary acting on their behalf to aggregate information from different government services or to run software on their local computers for direct access. Such third-party-provided portals would be similar to some of the Web services that have become available recently for aggregating access to multiple e-mail accounts, online banking, brokerages, and other password-protected Web sites, but without persistent storage of users' credentials on the portals. The local application access example is similar to applications like Quicken or Money, which pull data from multiple financial repositories and aggregate the data in local reports. Government-run Web portals could be provided in addition to the base transaction mechanism, but such portals would also access the government service through the transaction mechanism.

The transaction mechanism would be accompanied by interfaces and mechanisms for communicating with the government portal, collecting the information, and providing it to the application or third-party information portal. The data sent or retrieved through this transaction mechanism would be described by common ontologies and data definitions (e.g., based on XML) to allow this interface to be integrated with higher-level applications. When access to government services is provided through a third party (or even through a common government-provided portal), security may be provided using proxy or delegate credentials. These confer to an intermediary the authority to retrieve data or enter a transaction on behalf of a citizen, but only for specific purposes and for a short period of time.

Government has historically provided data in electronic form, but often in formats that make it infeasible for all but a few specialized contractors to readily exploit the data. Application-programming interfaces (APIs) would also enable citizens and businesses to overcome this problem by using software that directly connects their own applications running on personal computers with government services. A number of technical issues are related to achieving this "lightweight" capability, however. These include protocol design, information representation and metadata, security and authentication, and digital libraries.

Crisis management and similar applications present some novel requirements with respect to e-commerce, including these:

• *Data escrow services.* Development of technologies and standards would enable escrow sites to be established where citizens could store important information that they might need to access in a crisis, as such information might otherwise be rendered inaccessible in their home machines. These escrow sites would, in some sense, be a personal analog of the disaster-recovery services already provided by commercial services for businesses, government, and organizations. Escrowed data could include medical records, financial data, family contacts, and other essential records. A principal challenge is that the escrow technology must protect the user's privacy while improving the survivability and accessibility of his or her personal information.

• *Circumventing normal controls on use of data that might have been collected for other purposes.* The serious nature of a crisis may override the normal desire and practice of not sharing the data. For example, tax records might be used to help identify individuals who were working at companies affected by a disaster. Information such as names and home addresses would be candidates for release under extraordinary circumstances, while other information, such as income, should not be released. E-commerce systems would need technology extensions that permit controlled release under exceptional circumstances and a means to discern when an "exception state" exists. Also, privacy policies and government regulations would need to provide a means both for allowing and limiting the extent of such emergency sharing, and for recovery of the data (i.e., forcing its removal) from its temporary uses after the crisis is over. As described above, social engineering is a significant risk that calls for a systematic automating of the emergency access rules. If such rules are implemented properly, the declaration of an emergency or a particular threat condition becomes an official action determined under a fixed set of rules, rather than something amenable to convincing some operator that such a situation exists. Blanket bypass of security measures should also be avoided in favor of a system that switches to enforcing an alternative set of security measures that are defined in advance. Modeling tools can help administrators understand the long-lasting consequences (for example, to privacy) of potential crisis-motivated decisions to change security policies.

• *Enhanced point-of-contact services.* The issue here is how one can extend directory services—in combination with the push technologies discussed above—to provide facilities for locating particular capabilities or individuals on an urgent basis.

The committee notes, as others have, that the government can play a leading role in promoting certain aspects of e-commerce and e-business, especially where the government is in a unique position to support the deployment of certain technologies, or where specific government services may be leveraged to improve the effectiveness of these technologies. Such opportunities include the following:

• Government as a certification authority or licensor of such authorities;
• Government as a leading player in deployment of other security technologies, such as smart cards; and
• Government as a standards adopter.

Models and Simulation for Decision Making

Technological advances have made enormous amounts of computer processing power available to government agencies. In particular, modeling and simulation technologies being developed today can be used to approximate extremely large and complex systems, frequently with hundreds of millions of interacting components. As representations of the real world, these models are unique in their ability to illuminate the systems' inner workings and predict the consequences of particular actions. Such models are relatively new additions to our arsenal of methods for understanding and anticipating how the world works. Making use of them for decision making imposes substantive burden of proof upon the developers and requires a confidence level on the part of the users. Modeling-research areas relevant to government applications include these:

- Underlying mathematical theory, including mathematical system theory, sequential dynamical systems, combinatorial and dynamical graph theory, and algorithm theory;
- Statistical theory and methods in areas such as statistical analysis of computer-based-simulation experimentation and modeling, statistical analysis of dynamical systems, and integration of statistical decision theory with cognitive action analyses;
- Computational methods, including optimal representations for high-performance coupled system architectures and learning and adaptive systems methods; and
- Because sensor data provide critical input to models and simulations, techniques for fusion of sensor data and model output, reconfigurable sensor architectures, and adaptive online data acquisition.

Software Technologies

Nearly all major information technology systems in government are "software-intensive" in the sense that the principal design risks relate to the capability to produce effective and reliable software. Software is the principal building material for information systems. It is difficult to design, develop, measure, analyze, evolve, and adapt. It is fragile and undependable. The reality is that software engineering remains a largely unsystematic craft, especially for large-scale custom systems. Few government software-engineering projects are completed on time and within their initially allocated budget.[7]

---

[7]These issues are discussed in CSTB, NRC, 2000, *Making IT Better*, National Academy Press, Washington, D.C. This point was underscored by the President's Information Technology Advisory Committee in its 1999 report, which, in addition to noting the potential of information technology to transform government, highlighted software as the highest priority for research attention. See President's Information Technology Advisory Committee (PITAC). 1999. *Information Technology Research: Investing in Our Future*. PITAC Report to the President. February 24. Available online at <http://www.itrd.gov/ac/report/>.

Software research includes not only development of software-engineering capability and the considerable range of associated activities, but also the design of systems-dependable software components (such as operating system kernels) and the development of architectural frameworks to support the large-scale interconnection and interoperation of components (see "Middleware," below).

The culture of the commercial software component marketplace, as evident from typical end-user license agreements, is that the maker of a software system or component offers no warranty concerning software function or quality. The persistent technical challenge of measuring quality promotes continuation of this caveat emptor situation. That is, even a considerable improvement in the technology of delivering and assuring higher levels of quality would not likely be adopted in mainstream software developments until the value of adoption could be measured and quantified. This applies also to large-scale custom engineering, in which challenges expand to include validation (conformance with actual organizational need) as well as verification (compliance with stated requirements, which may or may not be consistent with actual need).

Except for highly precedented systems, software-engineering processes in commercial industry tend to be iterative. Major vendors release periodic upgrades to components and systems, often several times per year. The vendors are thus able to respond to market demand. Large-scale government custom-development efforts often start with a "requirements elicitation" process, and the validity of the results of that process may not be understood until well into development—often, years later. For this reason, there has been considerable activity in the acquisition and regulatory community to support iterative models of development, in which successive prototypes are deployed in order to allow early feedback on particular facets of concern ("risk issues") relating to requirements, design, or underlying infrastructure. (More discussion on this subject is presented in the section "Dimensions of Risk" in Chapter 4.)

A principal concern in the development of government IT systems is the embedding of commercial off-the-shelf (COTS) components. This includes adoption of commercial components such as mainstream commercial operating systems and office "productivity" tools, as well as of open-source components such as the Linux operating system, the Apache Web server (which is the dominant server in use today), and the Mozilla Web browser. Many COTS components can be opaque and difficult to analyze, thus thwarting acceptance tests related to reliability and security. They can also be subject to rapid evolution—that is, from the standpoint of the integration effort, they are on fundamentally uncontrollable trajectories. On the other hand, failure to adopt commercial components may not only raise development costs and risks unacceptably but can also incur increased training costs (necessitated by unfamiliar and system-specific human interfaces).

With respect to the new generation of e-government systems, a significant challenge is in the rapid prototyping of new capability so that functionalities and associated engineering issues—such as security, interoperation, and performance—may be explored. Major new software libraries, both from vendors and open-source communities, are enabling this kind of capability.

Large-Scale Systems

A multitude of problems—including delays, unexpected failures, and inflexibility in coping with changing needs—are associated with large-scale systems, and government offers notable examples of such systems and their problems. Such problems have occurred, for instance, at the Internal Revenue Service and the Federal Aviation Administration and in numerous systems at the state and local levels. This situation reflects not only the size and complexity of some of those systems but the chronic shortages of IT expertise in government. The problem is growing with expanded use of the Internet, which has fostered proliferating interconnected systems. More robust systems would also help reduce the costs of IT staffs currently needed to support IT systems. And the importance of the problem is growing as people come to depend more on such systems.

Research should address deep interactions among system components and intersystem dependencies, unintended and unanticipated consequences of system alteration, emergent behaviors in systems with large numbers of components and users, unstable behaviors, properties of federated systems, and other phenomena. In addition to these systems-engineering issues, research must address operational engineering issues such as how errors are corrected, how security breaches are detected and remedied, and how backups or other robustness measures are executed. A research program including case studies of particular systems and methodology research on architecture, techniques, and tools could help address the difficult technical (and nontechnical) challenges posed in realizing these systems.[8]

---

[8]The case for researchers working on problems of large scale was made earlier in CSTB, NRC, 2000, *Making IT Better: Expanding Information Technology Research to Meet Society's Needs*, National Academy Press, Washington, D.C.

Middleware

"Middleware" is software that provides common services and capabilities that "glue together" software components into larger systems. Examples of middleware include authentication, journaling, auditing, database-modeling services, ontological services, indexing, visualization, translation, search and discovery, access control, and electronic commerce services.[9] In effect, middleware is software that reduces enterprise application development time. Compared to infrastructure elements such as basic networking or relational database capabilities, which are more mature, middleware has continued to evolve at a rapid pace. Its importance notwithstanding, middleware has, historically, not been an area where computer science research has focused much attention. How can the research community contribute in this area—especially given that many of the tough issues are ones of scale, heterogeneity, and integration that are difficult to address in a laboratory setting?

One role is through research that examines the properties of commercial middleware. Middleware often comes in the form of uniform "frameworks," which embody principles for component interaction. These principles are intended to have useful scaling properties with respect to numbers of components, distribution over networks, robustness, kinds of capability that can be supported, and so on. Frameworks in widespread use include the Common Object Model family (COM, developed by Microsoft) and Enterprise Java Beans (EJB, developed by Sun and IBM). Designs for framework systems (such as those just cited) can be analyzed by researchers from a theoretical standpoint. Analyses have revealed subtle flaws and design issues in each of the frameworks mentioned above, providing useful information to program managers and system developers seeking to make choices among frameworks.[10]

---

[9]Herbert Schorr and Salvatore J. Stolfo. 1997. *Towards the Digital Government of the 21st Century* (a report from the Workshop on Research and Development Opportunities in Federal Information Services), June 24. Available online at <http://www.isi.edu/nsf/prop.html>.

[10]See, for example, Kevin J. Sullivan, 1997, "Compositionality Problems in Microsoft COM," available online at <http://www.cs.virginia.edu/~sullivan/standards.html>; Robert J. Allen, David Garlan, and James Ivers, 1998, "Formal Modeling and Analysis of the HLA Component Integration Standard" [abstract], *Proceedings of the Sixth International Symposium on the Foundations of Software Engineering*, November, available online at <http://www-2.cs.cmu.edu/afs/cs.cmu.edu/project/able/www/paper_abstracts/hla-fse98.html>; and J. Sousa and D. Garlan, 1999, "Formal Modeling of the Enterprise JavaBeans Component Integration Framework," *Proceedings FM'99*, pp. 1281-1300, available online at <http://link.springer.de/link/service/series/0558/papers/1709/17091281.pdf>.

Another role for researchers is in contributing to the development of middleware aimed at specific government niche applications. The Department of Defense's High Level Architecture and Common Operating Environment are examples of efforts to meet perceived specialized government needs. Authentication services—both internally and for interactions with citizens—are another area where government leads in demand and has a role to play in middleware development.

Middleware is also significant for e-government research because it can provide an effective platform for rapid iteration in developing new system concepts, both functional and architectural. The library capabilities available, for example, in Sun's Java Development Kit or in Microsoft's .NET or in the tools available with most major relational database systems (to cite just three examples) permit skilled developers more quickly to achieve a level of functionality that allows new ideas to be tried out.

Organizational and Social Issues

As a complement to research aimed at new technologies, research on the relationship between organizational behavior and IT can also play an important role in realizing e-government capabilities. The e-government vision outlined in Chapter 1 aims to enhance rather than simply automate government's operations and its interactions with constituencies. Indeed, success in implementing new practices often requires simultaneous evolution of organizations and their supporting systems—it is not a matter of systems design alone. In addition, because numerous government activities bring together individuals to share information and collaboratively solve problems, a better understanding of the social and organizational aspects of IT use is critical. That is, research needs to be done to understand in a precise way the interplay of system design decisions, changes to business practices, changes in the operating environment, characteristics of the user population, and organizational outcomes. These issues become very significant when joint efforts are undertaken involving multiple organizations in order to deliver an aggregated service for a particular customer segment.

Such a broad perspective is in keeping with increasing appreciation of what CSTB's 2000 report *Making IT Better* termed "social applications." That report observed that emerging demand for "more and better use of IT in ways that affect [people's] lives more intimately and directly than the early systems did in scientific and back-office business applications" presents "issues with which the traditional IT research community has little experience." Successful work on the social applications of IT will require new computer science and engineering as well as research that is coupled more extensively and effectively to other perspectives—perspectives from other intellectual disciplines and from the people who use the end results, that is, the goods, services, and systems that are deployed.[11] The incorporation of a "social, economic, and workforce" component to the NSF's 1999 Information Technology Research initiative similarly reflects this new emphasis. CSTB's 1997 report *Fostering Research on the Economic and Social Impacts of Information Technology*[12] explores the rich research literature on social, organizational, and economic dimensions of IT use and highlights a number of important research areas.

Some specific organizational and socioeconomic research topics identified by this committee as having particular importance for e-government—research that naturally complements technology capability development—include the following:

- *Understanding the social and economic implications of e-government.* Where and how is IT applied in government? How can we assess the extent to which it enables improved and new government services, operations, and interactions with citizens? The goal of this research would be to understand general principles rather than to evaluate specific government agencies and operations.
- *Understanding how to use e-government strategically as part of overall government service delivery.* Research could help shed light on how specific technology capabilities relate to a broader strategy for how people interact with government.

---

[11]CSTB, NRC. 2000. *Making IT Better.* National Academy Press, Washington, D.C., p. 201.
[12]CSTB, NRC. 1997. *Fostering Research on the Economic and Social Impacts of Information Technology.* National Academy Press, Washington, D.C.

4

Technology Transition and Program Management: Bridging the Gap Between Research and Impact

Researchers, subject-matter experts, research program managers, and operational line managers participating in the workshops convened by the committee all pointed to the challenge of achieving actual impact on mission performance from research programs. Even under ideal conditions—when the research results are peer-recognized to be of high quality, when the user agency has a solid understanding of operational requirements, and when there is strong institutional incentive on both sides to accomplish the transition—success in bridging the gap between the creation of promising research results and the realization of effective impact may nonetheless be elusive. This chapter examines how systematic approaches can help research managers and user organizations collaborate to bridge the gap between conception and use.

The gap-bridging metaphor should not be taken to imply that the path from concept to product is linear or predictable. Indeed, many major IT innovations have followed paths with duration, complexity, and diversity of players rarely foreseen by the original innovators. This phenomenon was well illustrated in the 1995 CSTB report on the High Performance Computing and Communications Initiative,[1] which offered a

---

[1]Computer Science and Telecommunications Board (CSTB), National Research Council (NRC). 1995. *Evolving the High Performance Computing and Communications Initiative to Support the Nation's Information Infrastructure.* National Academy Press, Washington, D.C.

number of examples of well-established multibillion-dollar IT businesses emerging only after many years of research and development, with shifting roles of government-sponsored research, industry research, and industry development. Business areas considered in that report, nearly all of which continue to remain pivotal in the IT economy, include graphics and windows, redundant arrays of inexpensive disks (RAID), very-large-scale integrated circuit (VLSI) design, and reduced instruction set computing (RISC) processors (for an updated display of the links between research and major IT industries, see Figure 4.1). In each case, there was sustained government research participation, including both formative exploratory research and more focused attention to particular technical challenges. (Of course, not all research has this sort of outcome—some successful research has far-reaching socioeconomic or mission impact but nonetheless does not lead to billion-dollar industries furnishing products or services.)

From workshop discussions and other interactions of committee members with research-program managers, it is abundantly clear that government agencies that sponsor major IT research programs—such as NSF, DARPA and military service laboratories, NASA, DOE, and the National Institutes of Health (NIH)—have all evolved diverse cultures of program-management practice. Programs are managed according to management models and practices that are embedded in organizational culture and that may be highly evolved. For example, the DOD has a rich structure of technology-transition activities involving diverse contractors that enable it to hasten the maturing of critical defense technologies along the path from laboratory to operational deployment. This structure can be understood, for example, as a systematic addressing of the many risk issues (see the section "Dimensions of Risk," below) that arise along this path. There are significant differences in management style and approach among the various mission agencies and programs. (Box 4.1 describes two agency programs in more detail.)

In traditional basic research programs, research teams often operate independently of any particular end user. The NSF's current Digital Government program, however, represents an important first step in having researchers collaborate directly with potential end users. This kind of direct engagement enables researchers to understand requirements better, validate concepts earlier, and accelerate transition into practice. It also enables potential users to anticipate—and influence—emerging technologies. But regardless of whether an end user is present or not, transition issues must be explicitly addressed, and obtaining an impact in practice requires careful and flexible management by many parties. The teaming structure of the NSF Digital Government program can accelerate this process, but it does not replace it. The right combination of careful manage-

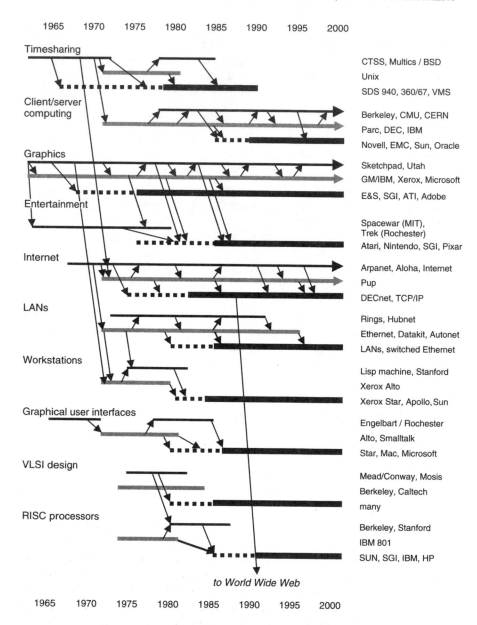

FIGURE 4.1 Examples of government-sponsored IT research and development in the creation of commercial products and industries. SOURCE: 2002 update by the Computer Science and Telecommunications Board of a figure originally published in Computer Science and Telecommunications Board, National Research

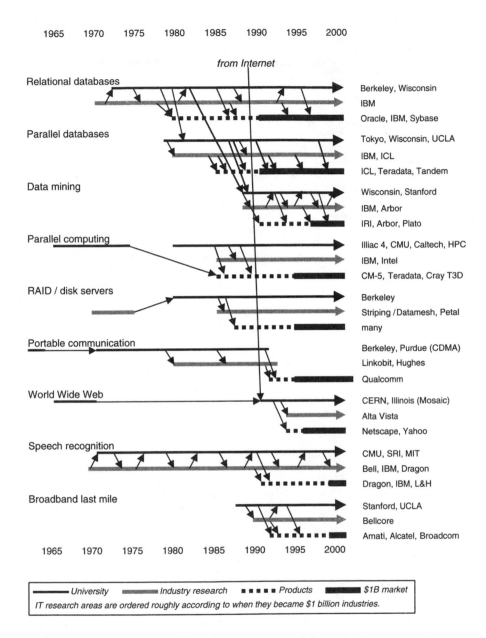

Council, 1995, *Evolving the High Performance Computing and Communications Initiative to Support the Nation's Information Infrastructure*, National Academy Press, Washington, D.C.

**Box 4.1
Research Cultures at DARPA and NSF**

Defense Advanced Research Projects Agency

For many years there has been tacit acceptance within the R&D community of DARPA's primary national role in certain IT areas critical to DOD in the long term. These include packet-switched networking, distributed computing, machine intelligence, software-reliability technology, and computer security. In each of these areas, program managers crafted engagements linking diverse participants in the research community, industry, and DOD according to principles that had been evolved through practice over several decades. This national leadership role enabled DOD to command the attention of the computer science research community, and indeed many computer scientists in universities have come to describe their research in military terms such as survivability, decision support, and situation awareness. Since the early 1990s, the strategic environment has been changing rapidly, prompted by the emergence of the private sector Internet, increasingly widespread computer-security challenges, greater military emphasis on asymmetric and coalition warfighting, broadening of the base of strong IT research universities, and a shift in the locus of innovation for many information technologies. Research and acquisition managers have attempted to adapt their strategies in response to these changes (with varying degrees of success).

National Science Foundation

At NSF, the principal criteria for research support are scientific quality and long-term socioeconomic impact. Perhaps unique to NSF is the emphasis on development of scientific foundations and a long time horizon, though other agencies, such as the DOD's Office of Naval Research and the Army Research Office, also accept a long time horizon when they consider a potential mission impact. In recent years, NSF has increased its emphasis on broad socioeconomic impact yet further, coinciding with the acknowledgment in the policy and legislative community of the emerging pivotal role of information technology in the national infrastructure and in society broadly. This is also a reflection of the increased attention to measuring the effectiveness of government programs. At the same time that it seeks to better identify the socioeconomic impacts of the research it sponsors, NSF continues to recognize that breakthroughs in "curiosity-driven" basic research in fundamental areas can have unexpected impacts in practice, and it maintains a broad portfolio of basic research in information technology subjects.

---

ment and favorable and even fortuitous circumstances may be needed in the operating environment of the recipient organization and in the markets for particular underlying technologies. Complicating this, the time scales can be very long—a decade or more in many cases—possibly well beyond the life span of individual research projects.

The NSF's Digital Government program illustrates that there is a natural alliance between researchers and end users. Both groups seek to identify new ways to address fundamental challenges in capability by stimulating new concepts and accelerating their definition and development. Researchers gain access to challenging problems and a real-world context in which to explore them. End users who participate in this process gain insights into technology opportunities and thus are better able to influence their future and accelerate the introduction of new ideas into their production systems. Despite this alliance, however, the transition from new concepts and prototypes to production systems and market acceptance can be lengthy and difficult. Below are examples of questions that might be raised by a potential technology adopter in considering a promising new information technology. These questions, which apply regardless of whether the technology has been developed within the government, at a university, or by a commercial contractor, illustrate how the challenges of transition go beyond identifying functional requirements and solving technical problems:

- Can the technology be effectively integrated into existing operations and procedures? Can it be packaged to interconnect with related systems? Does it comply with the interface standards that are adopted within the organization or by the integrators responsible for other major systems used by the organization?
- Will it be a cost-effective way of meeting requirements—in terms of both initial acquisition and total life-cycle costs?
- Are there fundamental difficulties in adjusting the human interfaces in a concept-demonstration system to conform better with organizational culture and practices?
- Can the new technology scale up appropriately to expected and potential operational levels? What are the dimensions of scaling, and how can testing and evaluation be conducted to understand the limitations of capacity and performance of the concept?
- What re-engineering is needed with respect to the prototype concept-demonstration system? Are certain capacity limits expediently "hard-wired" into the prototype, for example, in order to simplify implementation?
- What are the dimensions of dependability and robustness that must be considered in adopting the prototype system? Will it respond appropriately, for example, to operator errors or misconfiguration?
- Can the prototype system handle the full range of categories of inputs, or does it handle only a representative set? Are there hidden scaling challenges?
- Has the prototype been designed to support possible trajectories of evolution in the requirements it is addressing, in the systems environ-

ment in which it is situated, in the underlying technologies, and in the culture and mission of the organization in which it is used?

• Who will be available to respond to questions and provide technical support when problems arise or when adaptation is needed? What assurances can be provided to enable an organizational commitment to this new technology?

From the standpoint of the researchers exploring a new algorithm or systems concept, these questions may appear to be significantly less interesting than the more fundamental issues related to overall feasibility of the technical approach. This amounts to a division of both expertise and responsibility: researchers and their sponsors may focus their initial effort on the overall "concept" or the new algorithmic (or other) idea. But part of the price of success is that once these core conceptual issues are addressed, a diversity of other kinds of expertise must be applied to address adoption-related challenges such as those enumerated above.

A successful transition process must address a wide range of concerns beyond the "merely" technical—including economic and market issues, intellectual property and nonappropriability, standards, the "tipping" of the market in favor of a particular product or standard, organizational issues, and engineering and usability issues. At the committee's workshops, in the extensive discussions about the development, evaluation, and transition of new technologies to practice, participants particularly noted the risks and challenges of scaling and integrating new capabilities. But perhaps the most important lesson learned from those discussions is that transition cannot occur without broad knowledge of the technological and operational environments, including the extent to which those environments are affected by changing market conditions, standards, and other external forces.

STRATEGIES AND MODELS FOR PROGRAM MANAGEMENT

How can researchers, research managers, acquisition managers, and users develop successful strategies in this complex and changing environment? The sections below present an approach that is based on three principal elements:

1. Consideration and analysis of past programs, including both positive and negative experiences;
2. Use of program-management models, which facilitate comparative consideration of alternative approaches; and
3. Identification of proven program-management strategies by which

management decisions can maximize the opportunity for impact with acceptable risk and time horizons.

This chaper discusses two models[2] in conventional use in program management. Also enumerated are several examples of strategies employed by program managers in implementing programs to achieve particular kinds of goals. (The emphasis here is on long-term programs seeking a focused impact; approaches to managing purely exploratory programs are not within the scope of this document.)

Models play an informal but essential role in developing and managing successful long-term research programs. Little real data on research-program management exist, which means that managers generally plan and decide largely on the basis of personal experience and organizational culture. The models identified here are intended to organize and express concepts that are generally already present in the culture of program management in various agencies and organizations. The following two models are widely used, often in a tacit way, by research-program managers in articulating, developing, and managing their programs.

• The supply chain, or technology food chain, is an identification of stakeholders—and the relationships between them—involved in transforming a new technical idea into operational reality (see Box 4.2). Because this model is useful in understanding the respective roles and interests of stakeholders in the process of developing and delivering capability, it can help guide a program manager in identifying potential partners in an innovation process.

• The dimensions of risk are categories of engineering or market strategy issues that a program manager must address as a new technology or concept moves through the supply chain from an initial innovative

---

[2]Generally speaking, a model is a conceptual structure used to understand and predict phenomena that may be difficult to observe and influence directly. Models are abstract, in the sense that they omit details in order to facilitate expression and understanding of aspects of the phenomenon. Good models are expressive, in that they capture knowledge that cannot easily be gained by experience except perhaps at great expense or danger or over long periods of time. The validity of a model is the extent to which it has predictive power in the domains for which it is designed. Engineers, managers, and others may use a diversity of models in a design process in order to understand the various aspects of a problem, the design issues, and the potential consequences of particular design decisions. Qualitative and informal models, such as those summarized here, may be less predictive than a validated scientific model. The validation of these informal management models is necessarily informally based, and indeed all variables may not be identified. But for many disciplines of endeavor, including research-program management, this is the best that can be achieved with present levels of understanding.

Box 4.2
The Innovation Pipeline

It is well understood that innovation does not follow a neat, linear progression from research laboratory to delivered product; rather, innovation involves complex flows of ideas and people among the various organizational participants. Nonetheless, it is often useful to view IT research, development, and application as constituting an innovation pipeline that includes the following:

- Academic and industry researchers develop new concepts and technologies.
- Exploratory efforts made in partially realistic settings by industry, academia, and government agencies co-develop concepts and technologies to identify promising new solutions that combine innovations in technology and business practices.
- Vendors and tool suppliers develop software and hardware components and provide them to system integrators or to the agencies directly.
- System integrators, vertical suppliers, and vendors respond to requests for proposals (RFPs) and build (and sometimes operate) systems for government agencies.
- Government agencies develop and modify programs, issue RFPs for information systems, select vendors, procure IT systems and services from them, and operate IT systems.

This is a normative model for incorporating new technologies and practices into government systems and for improving services. As is discussed in this chapter, the interests and incentives of the actors in this process are not in reality always well aligned, which leads to a set of challenges for mission agencies and research-program managers.

---

idea to deployment in systems. Engineering issues include, for example, the scalability of a component or system, usability and adoption issues, and robustness of internal interfaces. Market strategy issues include, for example, whether to focus on adaptation of existing components to provide some new capability or to stimulate a new component market that packages the capability. The model for budget management used in the DOD for research, development, test, and evaluation addresses the dimensions of risk explicitly by categorizing funds used for programs (e.g., 6.1, 6.2, 6.3a, and 6.5) according to the character of the risk being addressed.

The following sections use these two models to elucidate a number of program-management strategies and tactics.

LEVERAGE IN THE SUPPLY CHAIN MODEL

Government IT systems are acquired in several different ways. If off-the-shelf components (see Box 4.3) such as operating systems, network components, and office-productivity tools can be used, they are obtained from IT vendors. If custom engineering is necessary (to fill in where off-the-shelf components are lacking), contracts are typically let with large commercial systems integrators. Integrators themselves often have incentives to incorporate off-the-shelf components into systems, thereby limiting the extent of new engineering. Larger mission agencies such as DOD, DOE, NASA, and NIH do some of this custom work in their own, internal engineering organizations and affiliated laboratories. In some cases, the custom engineering can be replaced by using vertically tailored products from domain specialists (for example, geographic information systems). Finally, in many government agencies, "seat management" approaches are used in order to provide federal workers with a base level of common, largely off-the-shelf services (desktop computer, office automation and other basic software, network connectivity, and support).[3] These provide both a core set of "productivity" tools and a common platform for custom and vertical applications.

In any case, the collaboration to develop new agency systems involves more than the immediate integrators and suppliers, because these organizations themselves obtain components and technologies from external sources. Each of the acquisition paths noted above involves a wide range of players—including hardware and software component vendors, systems integrators, niche technology providers, vertical-solution developers, government research-program managers, government acquisition-program offices, acquisition regulators, standards organizations, and other nongovernment customers—that have diverse capabilities and interests. Most integrators maintain significant relationships with vendors in order to assure a future supply of critical technology components that can address likely needs. A mission control system developed for NASA Space Science, for example, may include off-the-shelf commercial hardware in the form of workstations, servers, and network appliances, and commercial software components such as operating systems, servers, database systems, file systems, graphical toolkits, third-party domain-specific (or "vertical") tools, and networking components. An integrator will develop custom software components and "glue code" to provide the aggregate functionality and enable a flexible integration of components.

---

[3]See <http://www.gsa.gov/seatmanagement/>.

Box 4.3
Off-the-shelf Components

Very few systems now being developed are entirely custom-made. As their dominance of the IT arena diminished, federal agencies recognized that they could no longer afford to have vendors design and build systems "from scratch." This led to the notion of purchasing systems fabricated from commercial hardware and software—so-called commercial off-the-shelf (COTS) technology. The goal with COTS is to employ standard, widely used hardware and software products wherever possible so as to decrease costs and increase the likelihood that systems will be interoperable with other systems. The COTS strategy must grapple with a basic tension: even as government seeks through COTS to obtain a greater degree of flexibility that enables future vendor choice, vendors have an incentive to maximize the proprietary content of a system in order to increase the likelihood of future sales. Agencies thus face the dual issue of selecting an appropriate framework/architecture and managing the consequences of that commitment. In other words, once an organization has made decisions about overall system design, this constrains future decisions and limits which software products and vendor product lines will be compatible.

Recent legislation and regulation have created strong incentives for acquisition program managers to aggressively incorporate off-the-shelf (OTS) components as well as to support iterative acquisition models, prototyping, product lines, and other processes. Such incentives are appropriate in an environment of rapid technological change, shifting requirements, uncertainties in the life cycle, and demanding interoperation requirements.

Use of OTS technologies can improve affordability, reduce training requirements, improve dependability and interoperability, and enable the acquiring organization to "ride the curves" of performance growth (e.g., Moore's law) over the life span of the system. OTS components can be from commercial sources (COTS), government sources (GOTS), or open sources (no acronym yet).

On the other hand, the acquisition organization may find that it must sacrifice some control in the engineering process in order to accommodate vendor products. In particular, adoption of OTS components may force slight shifts in functionality that must be accommodated in requirements engineering and validation. In addition, there can be significant risk in verification and validation, since the acquiring organization may not have full visibility into the design or even functionality of the component. The acquiring organization also does not control the trajectory of growth for OTS components, and may indeed have little opportunity to influence vendors to accommodate special needs, given the breadth of their customer communities. Achieving a suitable balance in the adoption of OTS components can be a significant challenge, especially because the benefits of adopting OTS components may be harder to measure (though they may be greater) than the benefits of increased control.

The integrator will also employ tools and practices in the engineering process that, while not part of the final product, are nonetheless critical to the success of the effort. In short, the development of a major system involves a large number of separate but interdependent organizations—this is the information technology supply chain.

The research manager needs to have a nuanced understanding of the respective roles, capabilities, and interests of participants in the supply chain in order to maximize impact of a mission-oriented research program. The innovation enterprises and R&D strategies in the major mission agencies such as DOD, DOE, NASA, and NIH have therefore been structured in recognition of the scale, diversity, and depth (beyond first-tier integrators and vendors) of this network of supply-chain participants in providing advanced information technologies. For example, the history and, indeed, continued existence of DARPA illustrates the recognition in DOD years ago that achieving a desired stimulus over the long term requires a broad range of relationships across this supply chain of components and technologies. DARPA has developed a number of mechanisms (and made sustained investments) to engage with entities throughout the supply chain in order to ensure that long-term technology requirements can be feasibly addressed. These mechanisms range from sponsoring the development of underlying technologies and engineering processes to the development of measurement and evaluation methodologies that permit assessment of technology candidates.

In this regard, a strong parallel exists with the actions of major IT users in the private sector who work closely with suppliers in order to ensure that future needs will be addressed. Prudent developers of transition strategies for government research programs thus generally attempt to learn from industry practices and incentives, while keeping in mind that there are significant differences between government and commercial acquisition—for example, with respect to mission, public purpose, planning horizon, organizational structure, acquisition practices, the nature and extent of acquisition oversight, and regulation.

Mission agencies have an additional interest beyond their immediate mission requirements: taking farsighted steps to realize future mission benefits and adopting broad-based approaches to achieve broad societal impact. (A familiar example is DOD's thoughtful investment in the development and deployment of packet-switched networking technologies.[4])

---

[4]It is now well documented that this investment achieved a massive impact that went well beyond the immediate near-term DOD requirements. Nonetheless, these developments did not fully anticipate their pervasive use in public networks, and thus did not devote commensurate attention to the full spectrum of security issues.

It could be argued that these long-term and broad impacts can be a natural consequence of a combination of factors unique to government research management:

- The technologies were developed without a specific requirement to maintain proprietary constraint on the core enabling technical concepts, which permitted broad scientific engagement with the ideas; and
- The technology approach was designed to be vendor-neutral and to address issues of heterogeneity and interoperation from the outset, enabling broad participation from the vendor community.

Although not unique to government, there were two important additional factors:

1. The research plan addressed scaling issues from the outset, in order to address challenges of long system lifetimes and broad spans of deployment (potentially scaling up to millions of users within DOD alone); and
2. Managers sustained a focus on long-term vision and impact, spinning off nearer-term capabilities but without compromise to that overall vision.

WILL INDUSTRY DO IT?

An assumption in government that "industry will do it" may, for broad areas of IT challenge, be incorrect, despite the rapid pace of industrial IT development.[5] In industry, the return-on-investment calculations generally preclude innovations that are fundamentally long-term in character or that have broad and nonspecific impact. In the language of economics, many of these innovations are nonappropriable—the impact of the research results diffuses broadly into the technical community, and cannot successfully be confined to a single sponsoring organization. That is, the full value of the innovative ideas cannot be retained by any individual party—they create value for multiple parties. And because none of the parties can retain full value, their willingness to pay for the innovation can diminish to zero. This is characteristic of what economists more generally call public goods. Information technology innovations of this

---

[5]See, for example, the President's Information Technology Advisory Committee (PITAC) report (PITAC, 1999, *Information Technology Research: Investing in Our Future* (PITAC Report to the President), February 24, available online at <http://www.itrd.gov/ac/report/>), which observed that "the IT industry expends the bulk of its resources, both financial and human, on rapidly bringing products to market."

character include, for example, development of engineering practices that may lead to across-the-board improvements in reliability or foundational steps in methodology for the development of heterogeneous distributed systems.

A good deal of IT-related innovation yields intellectual property that can be packaged and protected; in other words, it is appropriable. But for a wide range of innovations, individual companies cannot make the case for investment because the value obtained may spread widely—including to competing companies. Scientific findings such as mathematical theorems or other laws of nature are not generally considered protectable intellectual property, and hence industry investment to develop them will not likely be justifiable purely from a competitive or return-on-investment standpoint. Some results of this kind can be retained as trade secrets, though secrecy may not be sustainable once they are employed in products and services. Examples include advances in the basic concepts of algorithm analysis, programming-language foundations, and performance estimation and measurement techniques.

Further compounding the challenge for the program manager, the technology sources for system integrators and consultant organizations are generally vendors, and less often, original innovators. Competitive advantage for a system integrator or other vendor often derives from predictability, risk management, and process, rather than from aggressive enhancement of capability. Indeed, acquisition program managers whose principal incentive is to achieve predictability of outcome rather than enhancement to overall mission capability may make overly cautious choices that do not lead to optimal long-term outcomes.

A system integrator's interest in research-generated innovation may thus be limited, as it represents a potentially disruptive influence on that company's way of doing business and could even undermine its competitive advantages.[6] However, there are numerous collaborative relationships between basic researchers in universities and their counterparts in vendor organizations, for such reasons as providing the vendor with previews of new technology developments or better access to educational programs and professional talent.

Universities and other research laboratories actually have a natural shared interest with the mission organizations at the "top of the food chain"—it is in these organizations that unmet needs (and thus interesting research problems) are first identified and, often, best understood.

---

[6]Remarks to the committee by Clovis Landry, Vice President of Technology for Lockheed Martin's Technology Information and Services Sector.

In particular, there is a natural synergy between the government mission to create public goods and the role of university (and federal laboratory) researchers in developing and disseminating ideas and having them evaluated and appreciated by colleagues. This synergy is reflected in the pattern of federal agencies engaging university researchers as agents of innovation. While there are natural processes in the supply chain that enable university innovations to flow into government systems, program managers can accelerate and enhance these processes by working at appropriate points of leverage. For example, government can support researchers in creating "prenormative" definitions for interfaces that can lead to standards for the delivery of new kinds of information services as a way to stimulate innovation.

The Department of Defense, for example, develops its most technologically aggressive concepts by engaging university and laboratory research teams. If the concepts have promise and the risks of further development and scale-up are acceptable, then the DOD will stimulate collaboration between those research teams and vendor or integrator organizations. The DOD invests in this participation in order to "buy down the risk" of commercial organizations committing resources, assimilating innovations, and developing underlying technological infrastructure in advance of concrete evidence of a market.

When university researchers do develop appropriable technologies, they can follow several possible routes to achieving impact, many of which involve moving into the marketplace. One of the most common pathways (even in difficult economic times) is the creation of start-up companies that provide vehicles for packaging and proving a technology and also for evaluating its underlying value in the marketplace. Successful start-up companies may be acquired by vendors—or, less often, grow into vendors themselves. The vendor thus acquires the packaged intellectual property, as well as the experience, validation, and contacts with early adopter customers. Alternatively, the intellectual property may be packaged and marketed directly to vendors by a university. Regardless, there are good reasons why a government (or private sector) research sponsor may promote this kind of commercialization. It can accelerate the transition of the technology into latter stages of the supply chain and thus into practice, at lower cost, while reaping the knowledge and skills of leading-edge researchers.

Another potential point of leverage for a government agency is to establish an organization along the lines of an incubator/venture-capital investor that can share financial risks in identifying, developing, and demonstrating new technologies. (This idea motivated the Central Intelligence Agency [CIA] In-Q-Tel, which seeks to invest in technology areas where both a CIA need and commercial interest exist.)

DIMENSIONS OF RISK

Risk (or, more accurately, risk exposure) may be roughly defined as the product of the probability of an unsuccessful outcome with the extent of loss suffered when that outcome is experienced. Thus, risk is high when either unsuccessful outcomes are very likely, regardless of consequence, or when unsuccessful outcomes are less likely, but with high consequence of loss.

These meanings are distorted slightly in the vernacular of program management. A research program is often referred to as a "high-risk, high-payoff" activity when it is attempting to achieve a major breakthrough, but with uncertain likelihood of success. Long-term basic research programs are generally intended to be of that type, in this positive sense: for researchers, a "high-risk, high-payoff" program has a higher likelihood of failure but a larger impact if successful, while a more conservative "low-risk" program—focused, perhaps, on achieving incremental gains in an established technology area by following routine scientific approaches—carries a higher likelihood of lesser impact. This notion of risk is almost always approached in a qualitative manner, as it is rarely the case that probabilities of failure and consequences of success can be usefully quantified.

How can a program manager think systematically about questions related to risk when very few of the variables of interest can be quantified and when programs exhibit diverse kinds of risk? In this section, several dimensions of risk are identified, along with some examples of strategies that can be used to mitigate the risks and thereby move innovations closer to adoption. This framework enables program managers to put names to risks and strategies and to identify the risk focus at a particular stage of program execution; addressing too many risk issues at once in a program can compound overall program risk to unacceptable levels. On the other hand, sequencing risks necessarily entails some "willing suspension of disbelief" with respect to typical risk issues later on, such as scaling and integration.

An example of potentially high-risk investment by government is the development of new concepts for system protocols and architectural interfaces. The risk derives primarily from a combination of achieving the technical goals (for example, aggressive improvements in security and scaling for the Internet Protocol) and achieving acceptance among stakeholders and impact on the mission applications. Box 4.4 illustrates how risk emphasis changes as a technology is evolved.

The sections below consider several kinds of risk issues that are relevant to research-program management. They illustrate the diversity of kinds of risk issues and the need, when defining research and transition

Box 4.4
Risk and the Evolution of the World Wide Web

An example of how risk emphasis can shift over the course of a maturing process is the evolution of the World Wide Web from its original CERN (European Organization for Nuclear Research) design. From an orthodox IT engineering standpoint, many researchers have long considered the original concept and implementation of the Web to be flawed in a number of technical respects. For example, unlike other institutional information-management systems (such as digital libraries), assets are mutable and identified by location rather than by unique identifiers (i.e., links can break). Also, HTML Web pages lack sufficient structure to enable effective structural indexing. And issues of reliability, replication, security, and naming, for example, were not fully addressed at the outset.

On the other hand, if the designers at CERN had been forced to address all these issues early on, very likely we would have no Web at all. Instead, the initial imperfect Web showed itself to embody a robust and compelling concept that was successfully bootstrapped into widespread use, even though substantial evolution and development of both the concept and its realization still lay ahead. This kind of history is an example of iterative development with sequenced consideration of key risk issues. A detailed historical analysis would reveal which participants in the innovation supply chain addressed which aspects and when.

From the standpoint of program management, all details of the trajectory of an emerging technology from concept to impact cannot be predicted or determined in advance; the environment is just too complex and unpredictable. However, a deliberate but adaptive strategy for identification and sequencing of risk issues can accelerate the process significantly. In the case of the Web, examples of such activities include development of the Mosaic browser at the University of Illinois's National Center for Supercomputing Applications and the decision by CERN to make the Web technology freely available.[1]

This bootstrapping is a significant program-management issue. The early acceptance of the imperfect Web meant that many stakeholders were able to participate in its evolution. This raised the overall cost of the evolution process, but it also distributed that cost and exploited early market acceptance. Conversely, overcommitment to particular requirements early in a process may appear to offer "lower risk" than an iterative approach, but in fact it may raise risk because designers are considering too many issues simultaneously and so do not have appropriate intermediate evaluation points. Indeed, in the case of the Web, the locus of leadership and management shifted considerably over time, ultimately diffusing into a community process. An additional lesson is that the imperfect Web evolved to do things that a perfect-from-the-outset Web might never have addressed. The imperfect Web did not support transactions (it had insufficient network privacy to carry credit cards or personal data) but was evolved to support this capability.

---

[1] The identification, separation, and sequencing of risk issues is the essence of Barry Boehm's "spiral model" for software development (Barry Boehm, 1986, "A Spiral Model of Software Development and Enhancement," *ACM SIGSOFT Software Engineering Notes*, August; and Barry Boehm, 1988, "A Spiral Model of Software Development and Enhancement," *IEEE Computer* 21(5): 61-72). Boehm's systematic development of this model for software development represented a giant step forward for program managers. Iteration without identification of the particular risk issues being addressed can result in what some researchers now call the "death spiral."

programs, to establish the particular risks to be addressed in program execution. For each risk issue, appropriate management strategies for addressing it are identified.

Evaluation Risk

As noted above, evaluation of research progress and ultimate potential for impact can be problematic in early-stage or exploratory-research programs. Indeed, some organizations may avoid long-term and exploratory activity altogether because they cannot adequately justify the investment—they cannot provide externally verifiable measures of the potential for ultimate impact downstream. This is a perennial problem, as there are a number of good reasons why a quantitative basis for research-program management continues to be elusive. Most obviously, many of the variables that matter are difficult to measure, and the lag from program conceptualization to impact in deployed systems can be very long, exceeding a decade or longer.[7] Even when considerable mission impact is achieved, traceability from initial development of concept to mission capability may be elusive.

In a number of critical technical areas, in which the measurement challenges are particularly acute, progress may be thwarted as a consequence. These areas include software reliability, computer security, the effectiveness of autonomous systems, and the usability of human interfaces. In large-scale engineering projects, there can be considerable evaluation risk with respect to life-cycle issues such as interoperation, evolvability, and reuse. In digital-government programs in particular, evaluation risk is present in the definition and development of infrastructure for major information and transaction portals, in the use of advanced collaboration technologies to facilitate intragovernmental processes, and in the development of software technologies to support and evolve highly dependable systems.

More generally, what kinds of approaches can be adopted to enable progress despite evaluation risk? Strategies include these:

• *Building measurement into research.* Delaying research until measures are developed may be an inappropriate management response, because the same understanding that yields progress often also yields mea-

---

[7]A mid-1980s study by the Institute for Defense Analysis examined software-engineering technologies and found that it took an average of 17 years for a concept to reach maturation and an average of 7.5 years after initial development of a technology for it to reach widespread availability in industry. S. Redwine and W.E. Riddle. 1985. "Software Technology Maturation." *Proceedings. 8th International Conference on Software Engineering*, London, August 28-30, pp. 189-200.

sures. Indeed, one management strategy often used is to challenge researchers to identify appropriate measures of their own progress as part of the research effort, and to apply those measures on an ongoing basis to their own and other work. This can include, of course, retrospective analysis of similar projects in order to identify correlates with various aspects of success.

• *Benchmarking.* In the absence of direct measures, especially in problem spaces of unknown dimensionality, benchmark data sets are useful surrogates. This approach has been successfully used in areas such as high-performance computing, speech recognition, image understanding, and text management. Well-designed benchmark data sets can help reveal the particular elements of capability within a set of "competing" technologies. Different approaches to a problem—speech recognition, for example—may excel in different respects, such as the handling of ambient noise, use of free microphones, speaker independence, extent of system training, and limits on vocabulary and grammatical complexity. This identification assists potential downstream adopters because it enables them to identify relevant evaluation criteria better.

• *Testbed.* Many research programs focused on achieving realism or scale-up along various dimensions create testbed facilities for conducting larger-scale experiments. "Scale," here, can refer, for example, to the size of a database, the number and skills of users, the extent of distribution or interconnectivity, robustness, performance, and other factors. Further, by creating a facility shared by multiple research efforts, costs can also be shared and experimental results more easily compared and evaluated. In addition, potential users can participate in the testbed definition and evaluation in order to ensure realism. This approach is widely used in major programs (e.g., DARPA Gigabit Networking and DOD Joint Warrior Interoperability Demonstration programs). The principal risk associated with the approach is defining the testbed project in a way that achieves realism while enabling research issues to be addressed effectively.

• *Gentle-slope adoptability.* One risk-mitigation approach is to design programs that offer a "gentle slope" with regard to return on investment—that is, increments of effort in adopting a technology yield increments of impact. This approach (named by Michael Dertouzos) can enable researchers working with early adopters both to make midcourse corrections and to collaborate with the adopters in defining evaluation criteria.[8] The resulting "early validation" can help reduce evaluation risk even when objective measures are unavailable.

---

[8]The idea first appeared in an unpublished DARPA study in which Dertouzos wrote, "The gentle-slope systems will have a few key properties. First and foremost, they will give incrementally more useful results for incrementally greater effort."

Solution-Concept Risk

Another risk issue faced by managers of a problem-directed research program is the extent to which the program should commit to particular solution approaches. Such commitments could include choices for system architecture (e.g., business-rule framework in a three-level architecture), measurement frameworks, technical approaches (e.g., neural networks versus other decision frameworks), or infrastructural components (e.g., operating-system choice). Solution-concept risk is an issue, for example, in areas such as improvement of information security, text-search capability, capability to integrate databases, or support for distributed teamwork in some operational domain. Underconstraint of solution approach can lead to solutions that are incompatible with the target environment. Overconstraint, on the other hand, can exclude development of innovative out-of-the-box approaches—such as RAID storage architecture to complement development of larger and denser disks—that may offer superior capability. When early projects were initiated in parallel computing, for example, a diversity of architectural approaches were considered, which yielded a number of different options that permit a number of different classes of problems to be tackled today.

One example of solution-concept risk in the domain of digital government is the development of technologies to model and remediate unwanted linking of databases (e.g., to prevent revealing identities of medical-research subjects). Solution approaches could include, for example, development of large-scale meta-models of released information, data-dithering techniques, and creation of surrogates for zip codes as geographic identifiers. Premature commitment to any one of these could increase risk. Computer-security research faces a similar challenge—it can be easy for a program to overcommit to particular threat models or security architectures and thereby be deflected from critical technical areas and a diverse portfolio.

Strategies for addressing solution-concept risk include these:

• *Mixed strategy.* This approach for exploratory programs is to adopt a diverse portfolio of technical approaches. While it is an obvious response, how to manage it for success is not so obvious, primarily because of evaluation risk. That is, a more constrained strategy may reduce within-program evaluation risk but increase the overall evaluation risk with respect to the intended impact.

• *Iceberg model.* Diversity enables individual efforts to accept greater risk while not substantially increasing overall program risk. If there is an expectation that not all research efforts will yield impact—if local failures can be tolerated—then greater risks can be taken, leading potentially to greater levels of innovation. A supporting organizational culture is prerequisite to success in adopting this model. DARPA and NSF, for example, have followed this model in certain critical technical areas, with considerable success. These agencies understand that too-aggressive management at this stage could inhibit the exploratory nature of this activity and prematurely eliminate promising approaches. This approach may be adopted by researchers as well as funding agencies: a principal investigator may consider many possible approaches to a problem before selecting a subset for more focused effort. This approach can be applied iteratively, following a "progressive deepening" strategy.

• *Avoid overmanagement.* Project managers may be tempted to constrain solution concepts prematurely in order to obtain a more linear program execution model with predictable milestones. This optimization in favor of near-term predictability may actually increase overall solution concept risk because it compresses or eliminates the exploratory phases critical to the invention or identification of new solution concepts. Unless a solution concept is clearly understood in advance, program managers need to balance visibility and predictability (and hence measurability) with the fostering of exploratory and creative activity.

Problem-Concept Risk

Often the perceived gaps in capability are not the actual gaps. An organization may identify as a technology challenge what is in fact a challenge in process, organizational structure, or technological-legacy management. That is, risk is associated with the correct identification of requirements to be addressed (validation). For example, when designing a system to facilitate information sharing in an organization, the real challenge may in fact derive from organizational culture rather than from technological impediment. Or, an effective solution may need to address organizational culture factors and technological factors.

Sometimes the difficulty is not in requirements elicitation but rather in fluidity of requirements. Consider, for example, the design of command-and-control systems for use in crisis management or military operations. There are important interactions between the capabilities of available communication and collaboration technologies and the processes and physical organization of command posts. If aggressive innovation is sought in command-and-control capability, constraining the technical focus to address communications capabilities within existing organizational and physical structures may fail to deliver sufficiently innovative results and may indeed reinforce older, less-effective practices. On the other hand, an overly broad focus may not yield meaningful results. Identifying the right scope of research focus is thus pivotal in effective program design.

Examples of areas of potential problem-concept risk in digital-government programs include new command-and-control capabilities for crisis management, statistical-analysis support for nonexpert users of government statistical data, and database interoperation support for rapidly linking geographical databases to support crisis response.

Strategies for addressing problem-concept risk include these:

• *Wizard of Oz.* Even when a research challenge is appropriately scoped, there can be significant difficulties in designing a program that enables rapid and graceful coevolution of technology and its context of use. In particular, naïve iterative approaches can yield, at best, long validation cycles and, at worst, divergence from goals. The so-called Wizard of Oz approach involves the creation of system mock-ups that do not necessarily embody real capability but that can nonetheless enable potential adopters to experiment with concepts of operation. The early validation received from experiences with the mock-ups can reduce problem-concept risk and focus technology development efforts. The mock-ups also help researchers communicate with potential adopters by providing a concrete instantiation of concepts; where appropriate, they may also serve as surrogates for formal specification of requirements or technological capabilities. The Wizard of Oz tactic thus also addresses risks related to evaluation, integration, and usability.

• *Double Helix.* As potential users gain experience with new capabilities, the problem concept may shift in response to that experience. For example, the use of collaborative-filtering technologies has had significant effects on concepts of operation for electronic-commerce sites. In the Double Helix approach, a coevolution of operational concepts and technology concepts occurs. Close collaboration of technical researchers and subject-matter experts may, after several iterations, yield simultaneous innovation in both operational concept and underlying technology. Also, validation can be enhanced through ongoing empirical assessment of such coevolution. This approach has been applied with some success in the DARPA Command Post of the Future (CPOF) program, particularly in identifying and evaluating new approaches to visualization and collaboration in midechelon military command posts.

Integration and Adoption Risk

Can the technologies developed within a program be effectively integrated into an intended systems or organizational context? Answering this question requires consideration of issues ranging from interoperation to usability. For example, wearable computer systems used in systems-maintenance applications need to be integrated with evolving practices and systems for documentation management and maintenance reporting. This could be called "business process adaptation risk." While certain adoption risks must be addressed early in a research effort, addressing too many of them too early can multiply risk and impede accomplishment.

Integration risk is a significant factor for many (and perhaps most) digital-government research projects. Many new capabilities must be integrated with evolving commercial components as well as with custom-integrated government IT solutions. In other words, both the target environment and the base technological infrastructure are rapidly moving targets.

Many of the strategies mentioned above are used to address adoption risks. In addition, the following specific strategies apply:

• *Pipeline.* The pipeline model, often used in long-lived research programs focused on strategic challenges, embraces a portfolio of research efforts that span a range of levels of technological maturity. Achieving that broad span may entail working with multiple stages of the innovation supply chain—basic researchers, exploratory-development teams, companies developing new products, and companies integrating systems, among others. This approach was used with success in the DARPA Strategic Computing program in the 1980s. The program followed a "pyramid" model that encompassed simultaneous work on generic enabling technologies, multipurpose applications infrastructure, and aggressive experimental applications.

• *Producer-consumer connection.* One of the features of the multiagency High Performance Computing and Communications program (HPCC) of the 1990s was the direct connection it established between computational scientists and engineers and the developers of advanced high-performance computing and communications systems. The connection enabled system developers to get early validation and feedback from users (see the subsection "Evaluation Risk," above), and it enabled the users to gain experience and assess scalability issues for emerging platforms. The program accomplished this by seeding the market—"buying down risk" on both sides, by assisting users in acquiring aggressive systems and assisting developers in maturing concepts so that they could sustain external evaluation. This is analogous to, but not the same as, the alignment of end users and innovators in mission programs, including NSF's Digital Government program. The distinction is that the producer-consumer model is focused on building links in the supply chain, while the NSF Digital Government program emphasizes directly connecting the producer and consumer. Producer-consumer connection issues also arise when organiza-

---

Box 4.5
Using a Clearinghouse to Assimilate New IT in Crisis Response

How can the introduction and use of new technologies in the immediate response to a crisis be managed so as to maximize their availability and better use the talents of emergency staff? One idea that emerged from the committee's consideration of crisis management is to attach a clearinghouse function to emergency operations centers that are generally established to respond to crisis situations.

A clearinghouse would help systematize the introduction of technology into crisis response activities (an effort that is frequently haphazard today) and help promote effective use of information technology by technical specialists and emergency managers during response to and recovery from disasters. The clearinghouse would provide a single point of contact for easy exchange of information among technology companies, researchers, emergency managers, and practitioners and provide a check-in and check-out point for all technology vendors and researchers at the incident scene. It would also help direct vendors, researchers, and observers away from overburdened local government officials and toward the specific areas of need. The clearinghouse would allow for a more coherent and methodical investigation of all disaster impacts, the gathering of "perishable" data, and the tracking of all field investigations. It would help ensure that all areas had been thoroughly explored for resource needs. Further, it would facilitate documentation of findings and observations and provide all investigators with updated information on damage, through daily briefings and reports. The clearinghouse should be as close to the affected area as possible, while still providing the necessary space and support services. It should be located so that it affords access to the emergency operations center, although physical proximity may not be as important as electronic connectivity.

---

tions seek to rapidly acquire technology to support ad hoc needs, as occurs in crisis response (see Box 4.5).

• *Common architecture.* Interoperation risk can be reduced considerably by adopting common architectural frameworks and interface specifications. When the commonalities are well chosen, system- or component-specific interoperation challenges are replaced by framework compliance. Widely adopted frameworks—for example, mainstream commercial application programming interfaces (APIs)—can provide significant interoperation benefit in mission systems. Conversely, poor choices in frameworks can result in exclusion of mainstream components, high costs of integration and, when framework technical characteristics have not been fully evaluated, high risks both at the component and system levels. Because of network externalities, frameworks must be evaluated on the basis of technical criteria, market acceptance, and potential trajectory.[9] The

---

[9]These economic effects are discussed in depth in Carl Shapiro and Hal R. Varian, 1998, *Information Rules: A Strategic Guide to the Network Economy*, Harvard Business School Press, Cambridge, Mass.

point is that the system architecture can itself be a source of risk, which is appropriate when architectural exploration is a program focus.

• *Framework building.* Introducing a new protocol or architectural framework shifts emphasis in a research program from particular realizations of capability to the service interface through which it is delivered. This approach was used in the early days of the Arpanet in order to ensure that issues of scaling and heterogeneity were addressed from the outset. It is a risky approach, however, because protocols, interfaces, and other commonalities only have impact if they are widely adopted. In order to drive down the risks of adoption, specific tactics are used. For example, both the Internet Engineering Task Force and the World Wide Web Consortium generally require reference implementations to exist before a commonality can be considered for potential adoption. Introduction of service interfaces into existing prototype systems can be a successful strategy to reduce the costs and risks of entry for new participants. This was, for example, the goal of the Defense Modeling and Simulation Office (DMSO) when it introduced the HLA protocol in the early days of the Defense Simulation program. The risks of this effort were considered acceptable because existing prototypes provided evidence of value and capability, enabling a more direct focus on interoperation and scaling up. In the early days of the International Organization for Standardization's Open Systems Interconnect (OSI) network architecture effort, uptake was slowed by the absence of compelling evidence of feasibility and value.

• *Scaffolding.* Interoperation risk at the system level can be addressed through the creation of scaffolded components. In scaffolding, a common technique in component-oriented system design, missing components are "stubbed out" with relatively trivial placeholder components that have limited functionality. This enables partial early validation of compliance with internal protocols and interfaces (APIs).

Moore's Law Risk

Several years of effort may be required to develop prototypes and evaluation systems that embody a new IT concept. Few IT implementations are insensitive to the performance of underlying technologies. Improvements in processor speed, network capacity, storage capacity, manufacturability and economies of scale, and infrastructural reliability can enable significant new approaches, for example, to capability, architecture, and usability. Researchers can anticipate the improvements likely to occur over the lifetime of a research program by extrapolating infrastructural capability according to Moore's law and its analogs. If the matured concept is deployed 3 years after program initiation, for instance, the conventionally deployed platforms at that future time could be more than four times as powerful as those generally used when the research program was initiated.

To enable researchers to anticipate these changes, research-program managers sometimes employ a tactic of "living in the future," in which unusually high-performance platforms are deployed to researchers in order to enable them to gain experience with the targeted future platforms. This is sometimes also called "leading the receiver," because of the analogy to a football quarterback throwing the ball to the expected location of the wide receiver, even though the receiver may be far from that location when the throw is initiated. The tactic has been applied successfully in programs for computational science, information visualization, and applications for high-performance networking. In digital government, this approach could be used, for example, to experiment with the use by census takers of low-cost wireless handheld devices (now emerging in the marketplace), with speech interfaces for use in crisis management, or with very-high-performance network links available in rapidly deployed field settings for crisis management.

Reliability and Usability Risks

Many IT applications require high levels of assurance of system availability, of data confidentiality and integrity, of design compliance to laws or regulations, or of correctness of design and implementation with respect to safety or functional properties. This is particularly true for mission-specific government applications, and across a wide spectrum of government sectors ranging from health care, social security, and statistical data to aerospace, defense, and energy. The experience of highly reliable systems development is that users must sacrifice capability, flexibility, interoperation, and performance in order to achieve high levels of reliability—which includes fault tolerance, security, robustness in the face of component failure, and many other attributes. With improvements in reliability practices, the extent of this sacrifice can be reduced. Conversely, requirements for reliability can force program managers to scale back ambitions for capability, performance, and even usability. Usability poses similar challenges. All Internet users have had the frustrating experience of attempting to extract information or conduct transactions through poorly designed Web sites. In applications in which government information and transactions are made available to citizens, the need to provide broad access to a widely diverse population creates enormous challenges in achieving usable designs. Usability challenges are also faced in systems designed for internal use—for example, crisis management applications intended for use by professionals who may be in a state of stress when interacting with the system.

When designing a research program that is addressing a particular capability challenge, an important early decision is when and how to take on usability issues. There is growing evidence, for example, that the overall architecture of a system can influence the ability to create usable human interfaces.[10] In addition, poor usability may deter potential adopters even when the underlying technology has considerable merit.

Early attention to these issues may not be enough, however. Certain product attributes, especially those related to reliability and usability, are multifaceted issues that must be considered at every stage of the engineering process. Reliability in particular must be addressed during system conceptualization, design, development, evaluation, integration, and evolution.

Planning Risks

This section on "Dimensions of Risk" has illustrated and partially enumerated the dimensions of risk that might be addressed in a mission-focused research program and some of the strategies and tactics conventionally used to address them. Of course, these and other kinds of risks may be present to different degrees, depending on the particular research challenges being addressed. Regardless, it is clear that successful program designs incorporate, if only tacitly, an identification of the critical risk elements, indicating which ones are the primary drivers and which others can be safely deferred for later consideration. A full identification of risks does not imply that they should all be addressed in the scope of a program—rather, it can help a manager understand, and later communicate, how transition steps might be taken by others once results start to emerge from the program.

In addition to identification of the risks, the sequencing of risks to be considered can also be a risk issue: an overambitious program design that takes on too many risk dimensions at once effectively multiplies overall program risk and lessens the chance of overall success. This challenge of sequencing the risks may best be addressed by drawing on experience in research, engineering, evaluation, and operational settings, where the full range of risk issues can be best identified. Questions include how the risk dimensions interact, and which risk issues can be addressed in parallel and which must be done sequentially.

---

[10]Leonard J. Bass and Bonnie E. John. 2001. "Supporting Usability Through Software Architecture," *IEEE Computer* 34(10):113-115.

SUMMARY

While there can be no recipes for success in program management, this chapter suggests some models and principles that may be usefully applied by a program manager in seeking innovation in government applications. Most importantly, a program manager may benefit from understanding the challenge of achieving a particular innovation in the framework of the two principal models identified in this chapter—the supply chain model and the risk-identification model. This understanding may be developed and applied in a process that includes, for example, steps such as the following:

- Identify the desired innovation and the stakeholders in successfully achieving it.
- Identify the horizon (time available to achieve the operational impact) and the overall risk tolerance for the effort.
- Map out the full set of participants in the supply chain that links operational end users with innovators. This includes, for example, understanding the readiness of the potential participants and the natural opportunities for collaboration.
- Identify the principal risk issues at each stage and consider appropriate strategies for addressing those risks.
- Identify critical points of leverage in the supply chain. Understand the timing considerations and other factors regarding the opportunities so identified.
- Take action according to the understanding gained in the previous steps in order to stimulate appropriate participants in the supply chain to achieve the innovation goals. Example actions: Invest to stimulate exploration or buy down risk, stimulate collaboration, and facilitate new standards.

Appendixes

Appendix
A

E-Government Scenarios

E-GOVERNMENT AND THE DAILY LIFE OF THE CITIZEN

Online interactions between citizens and government—local, state, and federal—are becoming increasingly common as more people and government organizations connect to the Internet and the World Wide Web. Individuals are already doing many different things via the Internet, such as renewing vehicle registrations, filing tax returns and paying taxes, exchanging messages with their children's teachers, sending e-mail to their congressional representatives and to the president, getting information on their social security benefits, and even paying for pet licenses. Some of these activities, such as vehicle registration, have simply become more convenient with the advent of online transactions; others, such as accessing government information, have been so greatly facilitated that they have changed from being very unusual to being commonplace. Such availability of government information, transactions, and people has just begun, however. For a glimpse of the potential impact of a truly digital government on the everyday life of an average citizen, consider the following hypothetical case.

Margaret Jackson had been quite satisfied with the local public schools for her two children, but one morning at breakfast as she was scanning her personalized summary of the news, she noticed that the school superintendent had announced that French classes were going to be eliminated at the high school because of budgetary pressures. Both of her children were currently taking French and were enjoying it, and she had been pleased to see them beginning to develop some fluency in another language. She was sufficiently upset by this announcement that she decided to look into it further.

The first thing that Margaret did was to learn the actual cost of the French classes by looking up the budget on the school's Web site; this type of statistical information was available for all aspects of local, state, and federal government, and could be retrieved using queries expressed in simple English (and several other languages). She then quickly worked out how much this represented in terms of dollars per year for every local taxpayer with children. Next, for comparison, she found out how much was spent on foreign-language instruction in similar school districts throughout the country.

Margaret then submitted a general query to all government and news sources for recent stories or reports on the state of foreign-language education in the United States. Included in the search's results were a couple of news stories in which the secretary of commerce had cited a report indicating that the lack of fluency in foreign languages was making it harder for American companies to compete with those in the European Union. The search also returned the original report that contained this information. Armed with the dollar figures and the report, Margaret consulted state and federal portals to determine which people in government have an interest in this issue. Her query returned the names of three individuals: one in the state government who was responsible for promoting exports, one in the U.S. Department of Education, and a prominent U.S. senator who had taken the issue on as a personal concern. She immediately sent mail about her local school's decision to all of these people, copying the school superintendent, the high school principal, and the state and federal representatives of her district.

That evening, Margaret received replies from the staff of the state official and the senator. They directed her to some new state and federal programs that were designed to support education initiatives and that also, in some cases, included foreign-language education. The senator's staff also mentioned that a pending bill being reviewed by a House committee would focus on providing support for foreign-language education. She reviewed this material and found that one of the state programs might apply to her local school district. She also read a summary of the pending federal legislation and sent a message to the chair of the House committee indicating her strong support and giving some of the details of what was happening in her school district. She sent messages as well to the superintendent and principal, pointing out the existence of the state program. She then went to bed, pleased that her actions that day might have made a difference in her children's education.

CRISIS MANAGEMENT

Scientists have predicted that there is roughly a 70 percent likelihood that a major earthquake will occur in the San Francisco Bay area before 2030.[1] Further compounding the situation, many residents of the Bay area have no direct experience with major earthquakes, since more than 1 million people have moved to the region since the 1989 Loma Prieta quake. What might be possible with aggressive harnessing of information technology capabilities for responding to such a crisis?

At 5:45 p.m. on December 14, 2010, an earthquake occurs without warning. The severe event, measuring over 7 on the Richter scale, causes 30 seconds of intense shaking and extensive damage to the built environment. A poll of sensors located in homes throughout the region obtains information on the intensity and distribution of the quake and indicates where the communications infrastructure has been disrupted. Highway camera and sensor data show that dense rush-hour traffic is severely snarled and indicate that 900 roads and many off-ramps and overpasses are impassable. The retrofitted and recently opened eastern span of the Bay Bridge does not collapse, but the eastern approach is impassable. Numerous landslides in the hills severely damage buildings; neighborhood roads; and water, gas, and electric lines along the Hayward fault. Hundreds of people die immediately. Several thousand must be rescued, and thousands are seriously injured. The Oakland airport is closed. The San Francisco and San Jose airports are open, but there is no way to travel to them. Railroads are also severely damaged.

Sarah Janello is trapped in a Berkeley parking structure, but she has a wireless mobile communications device with her. Though the voice circuits are jammed with calls, she is able to send a text message informing the emergency dispatch center of her location, that her leg is pinned down by a supporting beam, and that other people appear to be trapped under the concrete. A system linking all the information from local governments, state agencies, and businesses tracks the numerous damage and emergency reports, including Sarah's, and matches response capabilities with these needs. The priority list is fluid, updated automatically as new data arrive. Several other people in the Berkeley structure also report that they are trapped, so this location receives a high priority and a rescue team is quickly dispatched. To minimize the risk to the human rescuers,

---

[1]U.S. Geological Survey (USGS). 1999. "Major Quake Likely to Strike Between 2000 and 2030." USGS Fact Sheet-152-99. USGS, U.S. Department of the Interior, Washington, D.C. Available online at <http://quake.wr.usgs.gov/study/wg99/index.html>.

robots are used to locate the buried people and to bring them water and other needed supplies.

While Sarah Janello awaits rescue, she is able to locate other family members. She finds that her husband and children are stuck on the Bay Bridge but unharmed, and they learn in turn that she is being rescued. Sarah feels a sense of relief in the darkness as she waits to be rescued. Afterward, she is located by her family at a nearby hospital.

Using sensors and atmospheric models, the Emergency Operations Center tracks the dispersal of toxic fumes from the numerous fires that are burning. When a hazardous situation is identified, the populations at risk are notified of individually tailored evacuation and shelter options through a "reverse 911" system that employs both wired and wireless communications.

These sorts of scenarios play themselves out thousands of times throughout the Bay Area that day and in the disaster's aftermath.

CITIZEN ACCESS TO FEDERAL STATISTICS

Individuals want access to federal statistical data. They wish to learn, for example, about where and who people are, the demographics of different areas (e.g., information about schools, cost of living, recreation), what is going on in business and agriculture, what is driving prices in a particular area, or what to expect with regard to inflation and interest rates.

How far have we come today toward realizing this vision? FedStats provides a single portal for federally collected data sets and for documents based on them. Data sources and documents are organized topically and geographically across all the federal statistics agencies. In many cases, the available data are constrained, owing to confidentiality protection, but summary information and reports may be available. Still, one cannot make such queries as, How many people will be displaced if an evacuation at the 100-year flood line for Manhattan, Kansas, is required? Or, what would be the economic impact of locating a particular new business in my town?

Imagine asking FedStats 2020 the latter question. This might trigger a series of questions back to the user not only to acquire more details about that business but to learn more about that user: his or her quantitative/scientific literacy and visual/verbal/textual/cognitive abilities. Then, the relevant data, complemented by additional data sources where needed, would be "crunched" with the aid of models and simulations. A response containing the requested information both fully and in user-friendly form would quickly be returned to the individual making the query.

To realize this vision requires IT innovation on several fronts, such as representation of information, archiving and searching, modeling and simulation, and information integration. Subtle but important issues, such as the underlying integrity of responses, will also become key. For example, when the same basic question is asked by people of varying degrees of quantitative sophistication, answers must be consistent.

Taking the scenario one step further: imagine being able to get a second opinion. The local chamber of commerce has contracted with a small economic modeling company to give you access to a model that uses a different set of assumptions. Running this model using a portal to the company offered by the chamber, the model accesses the same underlying census and economic data that were used in the government's model. The modeling company's software is able to access the underlying government databases directly, using an application programming interface offered by the government to allow nongovernment computer programs to analyze the data in new or different ways.

CENSUS 2020

The decennial census is carried out, pursuant to constitutional mandate (Article 1, Section 2), to conduct a precise snapshot of the national population every 10 years. This information is required for apportioning congressional seats and establishing the boundaries of political jurisdictions. Many other government programs depend on census data. For example, the Voting Rights Act of 1965 requires data on race and ethnic origin at a very fine level of geographic detail. Although one could contemplate obtaining such information from other sources, no comparable or practical alternative now exists. How might the census be conducted in 2020?

Postal address might no longer be a reliable source in 2020 for locating and contacting the population because other means of communication and identifiers (wireless telephone numbers and e-mail and other Internet addresses) predominate. New geocodes would be used to replace the Master Address List used today to find the population. Satellite imagery, coupled with ground-based reporting using global-positioning-system data, could be used to locate, geocode, and define every structure in the United States and its territories. That is, a determination of buildings inhabited by humans, along with a distinction between business and living quarters, could be made.

Once the geocodes were available, the age, sex, race, and ethnic composition of each geocoded household would need to be determined. Assuming that geocodes could be used to link to government administrative records—for example, records on federal taxes, welfare, property taxes, or social security—one could retrieve information from these government records and follow up with more traditional enumeration for households without complete information. Also, the linking of this information would immediately identify the government services used by these individuals. An unresolved challenge is what methods might be used to obtain information on homeless and other groups that could not be readily identified or located by any of the methods described above.

Appendix
B
July 2001 Letter Report to the National Science Foundation

July 9, 2001

Lawrence E. Brandt, Ph.D.
Program Manager, Digital Government Program
Directorate for Computer & Information Science and Engineering
National Science Foundation
4201 Wilson Boulevard
Arlington, Virginia 22230

Dear Dr. Brandt:

To obtain input that could help inform planning for future e-government innovation programs, you requested on June 16, 2001, that the Committee on Computing and Communications Research to Enable Better Use of Information Technology in Government provide an interim assessment of the potential role of computer science research in these efforts. The committee was established by the National Research Council's Computer Science and Telecommunications Board (CSTB) to examine how information technology (IT) research can enable improved and new government services, operations, and interactions with citizens. The study is funded through the National Science Foundation's (NSF's) Digital Government program, which supports joint research programs between academic researchers and government agencies.

The first phase of the committee's study featured workshops examining two illustrative application areas—crisis management and federal

statistics—and concluded with the publication of two summary reports.[1]
The second phase of the project, which is currently being completed,
synthesizes what was learned in the two workshops, information gleaned
from other published work examining IT research and e-government,
and inputs gathered in the course of two data-gathering meetings and
supplemental individual interviews.

This letter is based on the committee's two previously published
workshop reports, as well as other relevant CSTB publications on the
evolution and impacts of computer science research and the application
of IT in government.[2] The committee's findings based on this work are
as follows:

1. Realizing the potential of e-government that has been demonstrated in early efforts will require addressing implementation issues,
resolving shorter-term technology issues, and conducting research on
longer-term challenges.

2. While government can in many cases build on technology developed for the commercial sector, targeted computer science research is
needed where government leads demand or has special requirements.

3. Providing a sound foundation for e-government and other applications of information technology throughout society will depend on
ensuring a continuing, broad federal computer science research program.

4. Challenging computer scientists to address real-world problems
in the government sphere can stimulate interactions benefiting researchers, who need access to computer and information artifacts and realistic
contexts, and government agencies, which gain expertise and insights
that can inform and improve their IT acquisition and management and
research results that can be applied in government and elsewhere.

These findings are developed below.

---

[1]Computer Science and Telecommunications Board, National Research Council, 1999,
Summary of a Workshop on Information Technology Research for Crisis Management, National
Academy Press, Washington, D.C.; and Computer Science and Telecommunications Board,
National Research Council, 2000, *Summary of a Workshop on Information Technology Research
for Federal Statistics*, National Academy Press, Washington, D.C.

[2]This letter report was reviewed by individuals chosen for their diverse perspectives and
technical expertise, in accordance with procedures approved by the National Research
Council's (NRC's) Report Review Committee. We wish to thank the following individuals
for their participation in the review of this report: John H. Gibbons, Former Assistant to the
President for Science and Technology and Former Director, Office of Science and Technology
Policy; Bruce W. McConnell, McConnell International, LLC; Arati Prabhakar, U.S. Venture
Partners; and Robert Sproull, Sun Microsystems Laboratories. The review of this report was
overseen by Samuel H. Fuller, Analog Devices, and William G. Howard, Jr., independent
consultant. Appointed by the NRC, they were responsible for making certain that an independent examination of this report was carried out in accordance with institutional procedures and that all review comments were carefully considered. Responsibility for the final
content of this report rests entirely with the authoring committee and the NRC.

1. REALIZING THE POTENTIAL OF E-GOVERNMENT THAT HAS BEEN DEMONSTRATED IN EARLY EFFORTS WILL REQUIRE ADDRESSING IMPLEMENTATION ISSUES, RESOLVING SHORTER-TERM TECHNOLOGY ISSUES, AND CONDUCTING RESEARCH ON LONGER-TERM CHALLENGES.

The emergence of the Internet and other technologies for electronic commerce has given rise to the concept of "digital government" or "e-government"—the application of information technology (IT) and associated changes in practices to foster a more informed, engaged citizenry and more efficient, accountable government operations. Among the key features envisioned for e-government are increasing access to government information, facilitating transactions with government agencies, making access to information and transactions ubiquitous, better meeting the needs of specific groups of users, increasing people's participation in government, and meeting expectations for advances in government-unique areas.[3] Constituencies include citizens, businesses, nonprofit organizations, and the diverse agencies of federal, state, and local government.

Ideas from early e-government experiments have contributed both to technology development and to the improvement of government's business practices. Among the most visible enhancements have been aggregated cross-agency portals. These Web sites provide users with access to information and services organized by broad topic and user constituency rather than by specific government departments or agencies, and often are task-oriented.[4] Computer-based tax-filing and inquiry-response services provided by multiple agencies are other publicly visible illustrations of positive changes in the way government does its business. Also apparent—in news accounts from across the country—are difficulties experienced by government agencies seeking new capabilities.[5]

---

[3] A 1996 report based on a series of CSTB projects examining needs at the Internal Revenue Service suggested similar goals, stating that "based on its work of the past 5 years, the committee strongly believes that the modernization of the IRS, including both business re-engineering and advanced automation, is extremely important. Modernization is necessary to improve taxpayer service and to allow the IRS to operate within an increasingly automated society, both of which ultimately ensure that taxes can be collected efficiently." (Computer Science and Telecommunications Board, National Research Council. 1996. *Continued Review of Tax Systems Modernization at the Internal Revenue Service*. National Academy Press, Washington, D.C., p. 3.)

[4] One of the earliest portals, fedstats.gov, is discussed in Computer Science and Telecommunications Board, National Research Council, 2000, *Summary of a Workshop on Information Technology Research for Federal Statistics*, National Academy Press, Washington, D.C.

[5] For example, CSTB's 1996 review of IRS modernization efforts cautioned that "the IRS has had serious technical capability problems that, in the committee's view, cast doubt on the overall success of TSM if they are not solved." (Computer Science and Telecommunications Board, National Research Council. 1996. *Continued Review of Tax Systems Modernization at the Internal Revenue Service*. National Academy Press, Washington, D.C., p. 4.)

In its examination of IT for crisis management and the collection, analysis, and dissemination of federal statistics, the committee identified a number of challenges to the government's effective exploitation of IT. These include ensuring the interoperation and integration of diverse systems used by different departments and agencies with multiple stakeholders and a significant legacy base; accommodating existing organizational structures that are difficult to rework to enable exploiting new opportunities afforded by IT; improving trustworthiness, including guarantees of information systems security as well as assurances regarding user privacy and system availability; bridging significant gaps between current practice and best available practices; and meeting specific technology needs related to government missions (see finding 2, below). Each challenge incorporates a mix of implementation, management, short-term technical challenges, and long-term research needs.

Technology transition is an important consideration when research is needed to achieve desired capabilities. The work of researchers may focus primarily on inventing a new capability, but implementation must address the additional challenges of enabling the translation of that invention into a reliable, working product or service.

2. WHILE GOVERNMENT CAN IN MANY CASES BUILD ON TECHNOLOGY DEVELOPED FOR THE COMMERCIAL SECTOR, TARGETED COMPUTER SCIENCE RESEARCH IS NEEDED WHERE GOVERNMENT LEADS DEMAND OR HAS SPECIAL REQUIREMENTS.

Although it can generally build on the technologies and services emerging in the commercial e-business marketplace, government leads demand in some areas. Research in these areas could help government agencies to better accomplish their missions. Moreover, properly managed research in areas of leading demand can stimulate commercial interest and development and thus enable government to move more rapidly away from acquisition of expensive custom systems, whose full life-cycle costs government must bear, to the use of off-the-shelf commercial capabilities. As a result of this process, government now can make use of commercial operating systems with process separation, multimedia databases, and packet-switched networking gear, among other capabilities.

Important Areas of Leading Demand

Ubiquity. Governments must provide services to all citizens—they cannot, in general, opt to serve only the easiest-to-reach customers or participate only in particular market segments. Nor can citizens choose which government they will deal with. Breadth of service encompasses the range of individuals' physical, cognitive, and language abilities as well as their education, income, and geographic location. Near-ubiquitous service is provided today primarily through in-person, telephone, and postal mail interactions, but e-mail, the Web, public kiosks, and other IT-based approaches are providing new opportunities to expand access to—and the accessibility of—services. Government, which must comprehensively address the needs of its citizens, has been a leader in exploring how to make technologies accessible, whereas industry has the option of focusing selectively to maximize returns. Research in areas such as human-computer interaction, information retrieval, language translation, and speech recognition and synthesis can help to increase the ubiquity of information and services. Achieving usability and accessibility requires that systems be used, and government applications may provide a range of contexts in which researchers can frame their efforts.[6]

Trustworthiness. Citizens expect government to provide assurances of security—which includes confidentiality (protection of personal and business information), integrity of information and systems, and availability of information and systems—that are generally stronger than those expected of the private sector. But what is desired may be beyond what the technology and practice can actually offer. Conventional business practice incorporates risk management, in which the costs of implementing security measures are balanced against the consequences of not having them—a calculation that certain levels of exposure can be tolerated for certain applications. Government agencies, however, are expected to adhere to a higher standard—no improper disclosure of personal information contained in statistical data, tax filings, social security records, and the like—even though government is also charged with releasing certain kinds of information, which may be derived from sensitive personal or corporate information that it collects, and making it uniformly available to all.

Trust in public systems is essential for public compliance with government mandates (e.g., paying taxes, completing census forms); equally critical is trust in the safety and reliability of systems on which lives may depend. In military applications, requirements for trustworthiness have led to efforts to promote "high-assurance" [7] technologies for critical sys-

---

[6]"Progress toward developing improved [every-citizen interfaces] will require basic research in theory, modeling, and conceptualization; experimental research involving building, evaluating, and testing of artifacts; and empirical social science research assessing segments of the population and how people actually work with different systems. In all cases, data, methodology, and tools are themselves targets for research or research support." (Computer Science and Telecommunications Board. National Research Council. 1997. *More Than Screen Deep.* National Academy Press, Washington, D.C., p. 2.)

[7]See Computer Science and Telecommunications Board, National Research Council, 1997, *Review of the Past and Present Contexts for Using Ada Within the Department of Defense,* National Academy Press, Washington, D.C.; and Computer Science and Telecommunications Board, National Research Council, 1999, *Realizing the Potential of C4I: Fundamental Challenges,* National Academy Press, Washington, D.C.

tems, and similar requirements apply to IT for transportation and health[8] applications, areas in which government is often in partnership with the private sector. Addressing issues related to trustworthiness involves intermingled considerations of policy, organizational behavior and culture, and technology. Computer science research could contribute tools and approaches for facilitating dissemination of information without compromising confidentiality[9] as well as for designing and developing systems that provide appropriate, comparatively high overall levels of trustworthiness.[10]

Coping with Structural and Legal Constraints in Government. Government, like business, has been working to create portals for information and transactions to meet the needs of particular groups of users. Frequently, this requires spanning organizational boundaries. Difficult in any setting, the associated modification of processes and organizational structure in government is often significantly constrained by legal and administrative strictures and may be further complicated by the involvement of state and local governments as well as federal agencies. Also to be considered are information-sharing barriers established legislatively to protect citizen privacy. IT capabilities such as trusted lightweight intermediaries that aggregate for the customer while dispatching components of the aggregate query or transaction to the various government entities involved in responding can help provide a usable interface to citizens despite the array of overlapping, partly interconnected agencies found in government.

Large-scale Systems. Making IT Better discussed a multitude of problems associated with large-scale systems, including delays, unexpected failures, and inflexibility in coping with changing needs, and it observed that notable examples of such systems and problems exist in government.[11] Many of the publicly acknowledged failures have occurred in government systems, such as those of the Internal Revenue Service and the Federal Aviation Administration at the federal level and numerous systems at the state and local level. This situation reflects both the large scale of some of those systems and the shortages of IT expertise chronic in government. The problem is growing with expanding use of the

---

[8]Computer Science and Telecommunications Board, National Research Council. 2000. *Networking Health.* National Academy Press, Washington, D.C.

[9]This tension is discussed in more detail in Computer Science and Telecommunications Board, National Research Council, 2000, *Summary of a Workshop on Information Technology Research for Federal Statistics*, National Academy Press, Washington, D.C.

[10]Computer Science and Telecommunications Board, National Research Council. 1999. *Trust in Cyberspace.* National Academy Press, Washington, D.C.

[11]Computer Science and Telecommunications Board. 2000. *Making IT Better.* National Academy Press, Washington, D.C.

Internet, which has fostered proliferating interconnected systems. And the importance of the problem is also growing as people come to depend more on such systems. *Making IT Better* points to the need for research to address deep interactions among system components and intersystem dependencies, unintended and unanticipated consequences of system alteration, emergent behaviors in systems with large numbers of components and users, unstable behaviors, properties of federated systems, and other phenomena. In addition to these systems engineering issues, research must address operational engineering issues such as how errors are corrected, how security breaches are detected and corrected, and how backups or other robustness measures are executed. *Making IT Better* concludes that a research program including case studies of particular systems and methodology research on architecture, techniques, and tools is needed to address the difficult technical (and nontechnical) challenges posed in realizing these systems.

Examples of Government Activities Posing Technical Challenges Outside the Commercial Sector's Normal Purview

Crisis Management.[12] Crises include natural disasters such as hurricanes, earthquakes, floods, or fires and man-made disasters such as industrial accidents, infrastructure failures, or terrorist attacks. Crisis management encompasses crisis response—the actions taken immediately in the wake of a disaster—as well as consequence management, which encompasses the longer-term activities associated with addressing disasters past, present, and future, including planning, preparedness, mitigation, and recovery efforts.

Computer science research can address the critical need for timely, authoritative, and relevant information in crisis response and management efforts. Meeting this need requires (1) a robust, high-performance communications infrastructure; (2) the ability to quickly deploy temporary but robust infrastructure when extensive damage has occurred; (3) the ability to access and compose information and communications systems operated by government at all levels and by nongovernmental organizations, sometimes on an ad hoc basis; (4) support for effective decision making and coordination in the face of uncertainty and stress; (5) tools to help overcome language and other barriers to communicating with citizens; (6) enhanced means of warning populations at risk, especially by providing information targeted to local circumstances faced by individuals or neighborhoods; and (7) means for adapting e-commerce

---

[12]Computer Science and Telecommunications Board, National Research Council. 1999. *Summary of a Workshop on Information Technology Research for Crisis Management,* National Academy Press, Washington, D.C.; and Computer Science and Telecommunications Board, National Research Council. 1996, *Computing and Communications in the Extreme,* National Academy Press, Washington, D.C.

technology and practices to accommodate handling the exceptions inherent in crisis situations.

Collection, Processing and Analysis, and Dissemination of Federal Statistics.[13] Federal statistics play a key role in a wide range of policy, business, and individual decisions that are based on statistics about population characteristics, the economy, health, education, crime, and other factors. These decisions affect the allocation of federal funding to state and local governments; the apportionment of legislative districts; and adjustments to wages, retirement benefits, and other spending. The necessary information is collected from a large number of respondents and at a level of detail sometimes significantly greater than that queried for in private surveys. The federal statistical agencies are characterized not only by their mission of collecting statistical information but also by their independence and their commitment to a set of principles and practices aimed at ensuring the quality and credibility of the statistical information they provide.[14]

The tasks of protecting confidentiality and ensuring trustworthiness become more complex when information based on individual records is made public and information records are linked across multiple statistical data sets. Linking, or the use of information integration technologies, enables answering complex aggregate queries, a capability that can be important to domains ranging from crisis response to epidemiology. But linking also enables the use of multiple databases to obtain information that, by policy, should not be divulged because, for example, privacy rules are violated.

In addition to IT confidentiality protection, the federal statistical agencies also lead in demand for IT that can effectively support users with diverse interests and capabilities in retrieving, integrating, and interpreting information drawn from the diverse and heterogeneous sources of data that statistical agencies provide, and for technologies that can support the scope and complexity of data collection efforts associated with surveys and the decennial census. In addition, government has a strong interest in and may lead demand for relating various kinds of data to geographical information. Accordingly, the Digital Government program has supported work in geospatial information systems.

Management of National-Interest Electronic Collections in the Digital Age. The federal government is responsible for three major libraries that play

---

[13]Computer Science and Telecommunications Board, National Research Council. 2000. *Summary of a Workshop on Information Technology Research for Federal Statistics.* National Academy Press, Washington, D.C.

[14]Committee on National Statistics, National Research Council. 2001. *Principles and Practices for a Federal Statistical Agency,* Second Edition. Margaret E. Martin, Miron L. Straf, and Constance F. Citro, editors. National Academy Press, Washington, D.C.

a leadership role within the national system of libraries and in the international context as well: the Library of Congress, the National Library of Medicine, and the National Agricultural Library. CSTB's review of the Library of Congress's information systems strategy[15] pointed to significant unsolved research challenges related to the Library's mission, including how to construct a massive-scale, decentralized, robust collection and how to deal with preservation of "born digital" and digitized materials whose format and contents are dynamic rather than fixed. The federal government faces substantially similar challenges in the task of archiving government records, an effort led by the National Archives and Records Administration, which has itself turned to a computer science research team for help in planning for its long-term digital archiving and preservation needs.[16] These and other governmental bodies play a key role in preserving national history and heritage, and computer science research can help with such aspects as the development of suitable systems architectures, automatic indexing, and retrieval of information in multiple media. That opportunity is reinforced by the multiagency support for the Digital Libraries program coordinated by NSF. Related and equally challenging needs arise in the management of massive data sets used for scientific research in areas ranging from genome research to space science.

3. PROVIDING A SOUND FOUNDATION FOR E-GOVERNMENT AND OTHER APPLICATIONS OF INFORMATION TECHNOLOGY THROUGHOUT SOCIETY WILL DEPEND ON ENSURING A CONTINUING, BROAD FEDERAL COMPUTER SCIENCE RESEARCH PROGRAM.

CSTB's *Evolving the High Performance Computing and Communications Initiative to Support the Nation's Information Infrastructure*[17] examined the payoff and key lessons learned from federal investment in computing research. The study concluded that the sustained, broad federal investment in IT research has profoundly affected the development of computer technology and ultimately led to many commercially successful

[15]Computer Science and Telecommunications Board, National Research Council. 2000. *LC21: A Digital Strategy for the Library of Congress.* National Academy Press, Washington, D.C.

[16]Moore, Regan. 2001. "Final Report for the Research Project on Application of Distributed Object Computation Testbed Technologies to Archival Preservation and Access Requirements," San Diego Supercomputer Center, San Diego, Calif.

[17]Computer Science and Telecommunications Board, National Research Council. 1995. *Evolving the High Performance Computing and Communications Initiative to Support the Nation's Information Infrastructure.* National Academy Press, Washington, D.C. An expanded discussion of the lessons from history is provided in Computer Science and Telecommunications Board, 2000, *Funding a Revolution,* National Academy Press, Washington, D.C.

applications. Many IT research programs not only reached their intended mission or science goals but also yielded long-term benefits realized in commercial products, companies, and industries and also in the training of a cadre of capable researchers. Ideas were often transferred to the commercial sector through employment or entrepreneurship. The history of federally funded IT research shows that problems motivated by government needs, such as networking and parallel processing, when suitably framed in a carefully designed research program, proved to have wide commercial application (as evidenced by the Internet, distributed transaction processing, and data mining). Broad goals were often pursued in order to infuse new thinking into the technology supply chain of vendors and technology developers for a mission agency. Examples of the success of this approach include process separation for security in operating systems (DARPA in the 1970s and 1980s), computational science (NSF, DOE, and NASA in the 1980s), and custom very large scale integrated circuit chip design (DARPA in the 1970s and 1980s).

The 1990s saw the evolution of computer science research programs to embrace a broadening set of applications and users. CSTB's 1997 project examining every-citizen interfaces to the nation's information infrastructure underscored the opportunity and challenge of developing technology that could be used easily and effectively by all.[18] Emphasis has also increased considerably on what CSTB's *Making IT Better* termed "social applications." That study committee observed that emerging demand for "more and better use of IT in ways that affect [people's] lives more intimately and directly than the early systems did in scientific and back-office business applications" presents "issues with which the traditional IT research community has little experience. Successful work on the social applications of IT will require new computer science and engineering as well as research that is coupled more extensively and effectively to other perspectives—perspectives from other intellectual disciplines and from the people who use the end results, that is, the goods, services, and systems that are deployed."[19]

---

[18]Computer Science and Telecommunications Board, National Research Council. 1997. *More Than Screen Deep*. National Academy Press, Washington, D.C.

[19]Computer Science and Telecommunications Board, National Research Council. 2000. *Making IT Better*. National Academy Press, Washington, D.C., p. 201.

4. CHALLENGING COMPUTER SCIENTISTS TO ADDRESS REAL-WORLD PROBLEMS IN THE GOVERNMENT SPHERE CAN STIMULATE INTERACTIONS BENEFITING RESEARCHERS, WHO NEED ACCESS TO COMPUTER AND INFORMATION ARTIFACTS AND REALISTIC CONTEXTS, AND GOVERNMENT AGENCIES, WHICH GAIN EXPERTISE AND INSIGHTS THAT CAN INFORM AND IMPROVE THEIR IT ACQUISITION AND MANAGEMENT AND RESEARCH RESULTS THAT CAN BE APPLIED IN GOVERNMENT AND ELSEWHERE.

Working on government IT problems offers researchers a number of potential benefits, an important one being access to the artifacts—computer systems, software, and data sets—that are needed in experimental computer science research.[20] For example, addressing the challenges of large-scale systems can be facilitated by studying real examples of such systems found in government,[21] and research depending on large, diverse information data sets can tap the wealth of public information resources generated or held by government agencies. A government setting gives researchers access to applications with a richness and texture typically lacking in the laboratory, and it diminishes the likelihood of constraints stemming from proprietary considerations that typify work in the private sector—ironically one of the reasons that the private sector can benefit from research on government problems, too, since the results will be publicly available. In *Making IT Better*, the study committee cited NSF's Digital Government program as contributing to the kind of researcher-end-user interaction that has become increasingly important to progress in IT, and observed that the government setting also lends itself to the recommended project-based organization of research work.

For government agencies, benefits stemming from research can extend beyond the research results themselves. CSTB's work on IT modernization efforts at the Department of Defense, Internal Revenue Service, Social Security Administration, and Library of Congress have all pointed to the critical need for technology expertise and leadership.[22] While there is no substitute for in-house information technology talent,

---

[20]Computer Science and Telecommunications Board, National Research Council. 1994. *Academic Careers for Experimental Computer Scientists and Engineers.* National Academy Press, Washington, D.C.

[21]Computer Science and Telecommunications Board, National Research Council. 2000. *Making IT Better.* National Academy Press, Washington, D.C.

[22]This situation was summarized as follows in CSTB's 2000 report on expanding IT research: "The difficulties experienced in getting these systems right show the limitations of current technology and of the skill base in industry. Government agencies would save money and improve their productivity and service quality if there were a better understanding of ways to reliably and efficiently design, operate, maintain, and upgrade large-scale systems and social applications of IT. Research based on government systems would undoubtedly improve the knowledge base for private-sector systems as well." (Computer Science and Telecommunications Board, National Research Council, 2000, *Making IT Better*, National Academy Press, Washington, D.C., p. 203.)

those studies have all suggested interactions with researchers as a means of tapping additional technical expertise, especially top-caliber research talent that is unlikely to be obtainable in-house or through the usual contract mechanisms. Thus, e-government provides an unusual opportunity for mutual benefit.

CONCLUSION

This letter provides an overview of key issues and illustrations of how computer science research can contribute to e-government initiatives. Technical problems arising from government operations have the potential to inspire important computer science research, and a well-managed research program focused on these problems can have an impact not only in helping to achieve e-government capabilities, but also much more broadly. The broadening of the computer science research agenda to encompass user needs and social computing issues argues for researcher involvement with the sorts of real-world problems found in government. In bringing together computer scientists and government agencies to tackle problems of mutual interest, the NSF Digital Government program has begun to demonstrate that potential.

Looking forward, a key question is how to leverage the research-management expertise of organizations such as the NSF, as well as mission agency research organizations (such as DARPA and NASA Ames)—and the results of the research they support—to meet e-government requirements. *Making IT Better* noted particularly that the leadership role provided by the NSF is essential for preserving the emphasis on long-term research and impact that is needed to engage top computer scientists and meet future needs. Government agencies, like businesses, have real operating needs that often demand short-term fixes, and these are not generally an appropriate target for government-funded research. Such problems, addressed in typical systems integration projects in which the problems and risks are better understood and managed, differ critically from broader, deeper challenges that can be addressed most effectively through collaboration with computer science researchers. Needs of an unprecedented character are most effectively addressed through programs that are carefully managed to engage computer science researchers in advancing the state of the art and participating in the development of solutions that are both realistic and appropriately aggressive with respect to the likely trajectory of emerging technologies.

Moving rapidly to address these unprecedented needs requires a strategy that incorporates not only the development of requirements and the invention of new technologies but also technology transition, organizational culture, and acquisition processes. Carefully designed research efforts can often anticipate these process issues and develop new concepts that are more likely to succeed as they are brought into government systems through acquisition, development and integration, deployment, and evolution. Finally, finding the right mechanisms for transitioning technology from research to government IT systems is an important practical challenge that must be addressed to reap the full benefits of research. The committee's final report will expand on these research management issues (and the other points discussed in this letter) in greater detail.

Sincerely,

William L. Scherlis, *Chair*
Committee on Computing and Communications Research to Enable Better Use of Information Technology in Government

Appendix
C
Workshops Convened for This Project: Agendas and Participants

WORKSHOP ON INFORMATION TECHNOLOGY FOR CRISIS MANAGEMENT

Agenda

Tuesday, December 1, 1998

7:30 a.m.	Registration and Continental Breakfast
8:30	Welcome and Overview
	William Scherlis
8:45	Keynote 1
	G. Clay Hollister, Chief Information Officer, Federal Emergency Management Agency
9:15	Break

9:45   Panel 1: Case Studies on Crisis Management

Panelists:
Nuclear/Industrial Scenario: *Albert Guber*
Earthquake: *David Kehrlein*
Flash Flood: *Eve Gruntfest*
Hurricane: *William Miller*
Moderator: *Eve Gruntfest*

12:00 p.m.   Lunch

12:30   Panel 2: Analysis of Information Technology Issues
in the Case Studies

Panelists: *Avagene Moore, Thomas O'Keefe, Jack Harrald, James Morentz*
Moderator: *David Kehrlein*

1:30   Panel 3: Information Technology Context

Panelists:
Information Management: *Barry Leiner*
Databases: *David Maier*
Computing/Storage: *Paul H. Smith*
Communications/Wireless: *Philip Karn*
Form Factors and Wearables: *Daniel Siewiorek*
Moderator: *David DeWitt*

3:00   Task for Discussion Sessions
William Scherlis

3:15   Break

3:45   Focused Breakout Sessions

Information as Needed (information integration, information management/retrieval, digital libraries, geographical and spatial information, . . .)
Session leaders: *Bruce Croft and David DeWitt*
Participants: *Paul Bryant, Elliot Christian, Gerrald Galloway, Valerie Gregg, David Gunning, Sally Howe, David Jensen, David Kehrlein, David Maier, Robert Neches, Edie Rasmusen, Tom Usselman, Lou Walter, Robert Winokur*

Information for People (information services at the
user level, human-computer interaction,
visualization, collaboration, wearable computing,
sensors and robots, . . .)
Session leaders: *Susan Dumais and William Eddy*
Participants: *Eileen Collins, Mark Deputy, Wayne Gray,
Eve Gruntfest, Ronald Larsen, Avagene Moore, Thomas
O'Keefe, Jean Scholtz, Daniel Siewiorek*

Commerce and Transactions (electronic commerce,
transactions, security, privacy, . . .)
Session leaders: *Cliff Neuman and Michael Nelson*
Participants: *Peter Bloniarz, Larry Brandt, Melvyn
Ciment, Stephen Crocker, Cathryn Dippo, Clay Hollister,
Frank Jaffe, Angienetta Johnson, Michael Swetnam,
Douglas Tygar*

Systems and Network Infrastructure; Modeling and
Simulation (software composition and assurance,
middleware and infrastructure services, system
integration and architectural issues, . . .)
Session leaders: *Karen Sollins and Sallie Keller-McNulty*
Participants: *Richard Beckman, Albert Guber, Philip
Karn, Barry Leiner, Joe Lombardo, Cathy McDonald,
Avagene Moore, James Morentz, Paul Smith, Carl Staton,
John Toole*

6:00   Reception

7:00 p.m.   Demonstrations

                Emergency Information Infrastructure Partnership
                Virtual Forum, *Avagene Moore*
                Transportation Simulation, *Richard Beckman*

Wednesday, December 2, 1998

7:30 a.m.   Continental Breakfast

8:30   Focused Breakout Sessions (continued)

10:15   Break

10:30	Keynote 2

Henry Kelly, White House Office of Science and Technology Policy

11:00 a.m.- 12:30 p.m.	Panel 4: Principal Information Technology Research Opportunities

Panelists: *Bruce Croft, Sally Keller-McNulty, Cliff Neuman, Susan Dumais*
Moderator: *William Scherlis*

12:30	Lunch

1:30	Panel 5: Achieving an Impact in the Crisis Management Community

Panelists: *Ronald Larsen, Earnest Paylor, Albert Guber*
Moderator: *Bruce Croft*

2:30	Panel 6: Lessons for Digital Government

Panelists: *John Toole, Bruce McConnell, Michael Nelson*
Moderator: *Michael Nelson*

3:30	Concluding Remarks

William Scherlis

4:00 p.m.	Adjourn

PARTICIPANTS

Richard Beckman, Los Alamos National Laboratory
Peter Bloniarz, Center for Technology and Government, State
    University of New York
Lawrence Brandt, National Science Foundation
Paul Bryant, Federal Emergency Management Agency
Elliot Christian, U.S. Geological Survey
Melvyn Ciment, Potomac Institute for Policy Studies
Eileen Collins, National Science Foundation

Stephen Crocker, Steve Crocker Associates
W. Bruce Croft, University of Massachusetts at Amherst
Mark Deputy, Montgomery County Urban Search and Rescue
David DeWitt, University of Wisconsin at Madison
Cathryn S. Dippo, Bureau of Labor Statistics
Susan Dumais, Microsoft Research
William Eddy, Carnegie Mellon University
Gerrald Galloway, International Joint Commission
Wayne Gray, George Mason University
Valerie Gregg, National Science Foundation
Eve Gruntfest, University of Colorado at Colorado Springs
Albert Guber, Department of Energy/Bechtel Nevada
David Gunning, Defense Advanced Research Projects Agency
John R. Harrald, George Washington University
G. Clay Hollister, Federal Emergency Management Agency
Sally E. Howe, National Coordination Office for Computing,
     Information, and Communications
Kay Howell, National Coordination Office for Computing, Information,
     and Communications
Frank Jaffe, Bank of Boston
David Jensen, University of Massachusetts at Amherst
Angienetta Johnson, National Aeronautics and Space Administration
Philip Karn, Qualcomm Inc.
David Kehrlein, State of California, Governor's Office of Emergency
     Services
Sallie Keller-McNulty, Los Alamos National Laboratory
Henry Kelly, Office of Science and Technology Policy
Ronald Larsen, Defense Advanced Research Projects Agency
Barry Leiner, Corporation for National Research Initiatives
Joe Lombardo, Applied Physics Laboratory, Johns Hopkins University
David Maier, Oregon Graduate Institute
Bruce McConnell, Office of Management and Budget
Cathy McDonald, National Coordination Office for Computing,
     Information, and Communications
William Miller, U.S. Geological Survey
Avagene Moore, AV/PM Inc., Lawrenceburg, Tennessee
James Morentz, Essential Technologies Inc.
Michael R. Nelson, IBM
Clifford Neuman, University of Southern California
Thomas O'Keefe, California Department of Forestry and Fire Protection
Earnest Paylor, National Aeronautics and Space Administration
Edie Rasmusen, University of Pittsburgh
William Scherlis, Carnegie Mellon University

Jean Scholtz, Defense Advanced Research Projects Agency
Daniel Siewiorek, Carnegie Mellon University
Paul Smith, Department of Energy
Karen Sollins, Massachusetts Institute of Technology
Carl P. Staton, National Oceanic and Atmospheric Administration
Michael Sullivan, BBN Corporation
Michael Swetnam, Potomac Institute for Policy Studies
John C. Toole, National Center for Supercomputing Applications,
    University of Illinois at Urbana-Champaign
William Turnbull, National Oceanic and Atmospheric Administration
Douglas Tygar, University of California at Berkeley
Tom Usselman, National Research Council
Louis Walter, National Aeronautics and Space Administration
Robert S. Winokur, National Oceanic and Atmospheric Administration
Rich Wojcik, Applied Physics Laboratory, Johns Hopkins University

WORKSHOP ON INFORMATION TECHNOLOGY RESEARCH FOR FEDERAL STATISTICS

Agenda

Tuesday, February 9, 1999

7:30 a.m.   Registration and Continental Breakfast

8:30   Welcome
                 William Scherlis

8:45   Keynote Address
                 Thomas Kalil, National Economic Council

9:15   Panel 1: Case Studies
                 Panelists:
                 National Health and Nutrition Examination
                     Surveys: *Lewis Berman*
                 American Travel Study: *Heather Contrino*
                 Current Population Survey: *Cathryn Dippo*
                 National Crime Victimization Survey: *Denise Lewis*
                 Moderator: *Sallie Keller-McNulty*

11:00	Panel 2: Information Technology Trends and Opportunities Panelists: *Gary Marchionini, Tom Mitchell, Ravi S. Sandhu, William Cody, Clifford Neuman* (moderator)
12:30 p.m.	Lunch
1:30	Panel 3: Study Design, Data Collection, and Data Processing Panelists: *Martin Appel, Judith Lessler, James Smith, William Eddy* (moderator)
3:00	Break
3:30-5:00	Panel 4: Creating Statistical Information Products Panelists: *Michael Levi, Bruce Petrie, Diane Schiano, Susan Dumais* (moderator)
6:00-7:30	Reception
5:30-8:00 p.m.	Exhibits TIGER Mapping System, Mable/Geocorr; U.S. Gazetteer; Census FERRET; CDC Wonder; National Center for Health Statistics Mortality Mapping Exhibit, Display, and Demo; Westat Blaise; Consumer Price Index CAPI; Census CAPI; FedStats

Wednesday, February 10, 1999

7:30 a.m.	Continental Breakfast
8:30	Keynote Address *Katherine Wallman*, Office of Management and Budget
9:00	Panel 5: The Consumer's Perspective Panelists: *Virginia deWolf, Latanya Sweeney, Paul Overberg, Michael Nelson* (moderator)
10:30	Break
10:45	Breakout Sessions 1. Data management, survey technique, process, systems architecture, metadata, interoperation

2. Data mining, inference, privacy, aggregation and sharing, metadata, security
3. Human-computer interaction, privacy, dissemination, literacy

11:45   Report Back from Breakout Sessions

12:15 p.m.   Adjourn

Participants

Richard Allen, U.S. Department of Agriculture, National Agricultural Statistics Service
Martin Appel, Census Bureau
Don Bay, U.S. Department of Agriculture, National Agricultural Statistics Service
Linda Bean, National Center for Health Statistics
Lewis Berman, National Center for Health Statistics
Tora Bickson, RAND Corporation
Larry Brandt, National Science Foundation
Cavan Capps, Census Bureau
Lynda Carlson, Energy Information Agency
Dan Carr, George Mason University
William Cody, IBM Almaden
Eileen Collins, National Science Foundation
Frederick Conrad, Bureau of Labor Statistics
Heather Contrino, Bureau of Transportation Statistics
Robert Creecy, Census Bureau
W. Bruce Croft, University of Massachusetts at Amherst
Marshall Deberry, Bureau of Justice Statistics
David DeWitt, University of Wisconsin at Madison
Virginia DeWolf, Office of Management and Budget
Cathryn Dippo, Bureau of Labor Statistics
Susan Dumais, Microsoft Research
William Eddy, Carnegie Mellon University
Jean Fox, Bureau of Labor Statistics
John Gawalt, National Science Foundation
Jim Gentle, George Mason University
Valerie Gregg, National Science Foundation
Jane Griffith, Congressional Research Service
Eve Gruntfest, University of Colorado at Colorado Springs
Carol House, U.S. Department of Agriculture, National Agricultural Statistics Service

Sally Howe, National Coordination Office for Computing, Information, and Communications
Terrence Ireland, Consultant
Thomas Kalil, National Economic Council
David Kehrlein, Governor's Office of Emergency Services, State of California
Sallie Keller-McNulty, Los Alamos National Laboratory
Nancy Kirkendall, Office of Management and Budget
Bill Larocque, National Center for Education Statistics, Department of Education
Frank Lee, Census Bureau
Judith Lessler, Research Triangle Institute
Michael Levi, Bureau of Labor Statistics
Robyn Levine, Congressional Research Service
Denise Lewis, Census Bureau
Gary Marchionini, University of North Carolina
Patrice McDermott, OMB Watch
Tom M. Mitchell, Carnegie Mellon University
Sally Morton, RAND Corporation
Krish Namboodiri, National Coordination Office for Computing, Information, and Communications
Michael R. Nelson, IBM
Clifford Neuman, Information Sciences Institute, University of Southern California
Janet Norwood, Former Commissioner, U.S. Bureau of Labor Statistics
Sarah Nussar, Iowa State University
Leon Osterweil, University of Massachusetts at Amherst
Paul Overberg, USA Today
Bruce Petrie, Statistics Canada
Linda Pickle, National Center for Health Statistics
Joseph Rose, Department of Education
Charlie Rothwell, National Center for Health Statistics
Alan Saalfeld, Ohio State University
Ravi Sandhu, George Mason University
William L. Scherlis, Carnegie Mellon University
Diane Schiano, Interval Research
Paula Schneider, Census Bureau
James Smith, Westat
Karen Sollins, National Science Foundation
Edward J. Spar, Council of Professional Associations on Federal Statistics
Peter Stegehuis, Westat

Latanya Sweeney, Carnegie Mellon University
Rachel Taylor, Census Bureau
Nancy Van Derveer, Census Bureau
Katherine Wallman, Office of Management and Budget
Linda Washington, National Center for Health Statistics
Andrew White, National Research Council